TYPES OF SECONDARY SCHOOLS
AND THE DEVELOPMENT OF
RELIGIOUS VOCATIONS

SISTER M. CELESTINE HOEDL, S. C. C.

Assumption College for Sisters
Mendham, New Jersey
1962

Nihil Obstat:

BEDE BABO, O.S.B.
Censor Librorum
December 8, 1961

Imprimatur:

✠ JAMES A. McNULTY
Bishop of Paterson
December 11, 1961

PREFACE

Environment plays a dual role in life. Passively, it provides a frame of reference for diverse phenomena; actively, it produces these changes. This passive-active dichotomy, however, is at best a logical division, without practical utility. To consider exclusively either aspect produces an unrealistic scientific "schizophrenia," since reality postulates the fusion of both.

The present research weighed the direct effects of environment on the vocation choices of adolescent girls in the referential framework of secondary education, thereby acknowledging the bipolarity of the term. Originally submitted to the Department of Psychology in the School of Education, St. John's University, Jamaica, New York, in partial fulfillment of requirements for the doctoral degree, the study is here offered to educators and administrators, who are perhaps already impaled on the horns of the current dilemma in Catholic education.

In the area of vocation, the impact of environment operates effectively in the various foci of human relationships: home, school, and peer group. Long a topic of conjecture, school influence has here been subjected to the discipline of scientific analysis. Resulting conclusions, therefore, might be considered more valid than mere guesses.

iii

TABLE OF CONTENTS

LIST OF TABLES

vi

LIST OF FIGURES

CHAPTER I

INTRODUCTION

Statement of the Problem

Christian education today faces its greatest opportunity and its most daring challenge. Never before in its history has the movement for its expansion been regarded with such favor. Never before have such vast armies of youth trooped across the thresholds of Catholic schools, nor have parents ever seemed so willing to assume the double burden of supporting two school systems. Yet the main protagonists in the battle against ignorance are too few for effective action in this area of human endeavor.

Burgeoning enrollments in both the national and the Catholic educational systems indicate the need for a critical reappraisal of teacher recruitment policy and its attendant problems. Bulging classrooms postulate a corresponding teacher force to cope with the untaught multitudes. The demand for teachers, however, far exceeds the supply. Not only in public education is the major problem of the moment the shortage of personnel; private and parochial systems also labor under the same stress. In the Catholic school system particularly, the need for religious teachers, specifically religious women teachers, is approaching crisis proportions. These religious women must be recruited from educational institutions, with the secondary schools a primary source of this commodity. Since then the secondary level can be shown to be a rich vocation pool, the present thesis is aimed at this area.

The secondary school system under the aegis of the Church has proliferated into many specific types, chief among which are the following:

(a) Coeducational: parish and diocesan

(b) Single-sex: private and diocesan

This classification is not exhaustive; there are numerous permutations and combinations of administrative types on the

1

secondary level. Circumstances, expediency, and the exigencies of the moment often dictate new arrangements. In the parochial system the situation as revealed by the research is fluid. Certain arrangements evolving from the directives of the III Plenary Council of Baltimore are gradually being replaced by newer forms of administration. A case in point is the small coeducational parish high school. Recent trends point definitely to its gradual decline and eventual demise as a type in the parochial school system.

Granted that the present teacher shortage is a major focus of concern for educational authorities in general and Catholic administrators in particular, and noting that the vast majority of teachers in the parochial school system are priests, Brothers, and Sisters, the investigator here offers a brief overview of the current status of religious vocations in the United States. *The Official Catholic Directory* for 1960 tallies 168,527 Sisters as compared with 53,796 priests and 10,473 Brothers. Sisters still outnumber the male contingent of consecrated service in the Church by a ratio of 2.6:1, according to these statistics. Yet the hue and cry rolls on: "Girls are not entering the religious life as generously today as formerly." Many Congregations of Sisters could belie this statement by releasing statistics from their archives which would reveal overflowing novitiates. Yet the deficit is all too apparent in empty schools, crowded classrooms, inadequate staffing, and overworked faculties. Many reasons might be adduced to explain the alleged dearth of vocations to the teaching sisterhoods. The more common and obvious have been cited repeatedly. It might be well, therefore, to mention a less obtrusive factor. One plausible explanation could be that the Sisters have been considered expendable and have been required to step into the breach whenever and wherever priests and Brothers were not available for teaching and administrative positions.

Accordingly, several thousands of Sisters are now teaching boys of junior and senior high school age who might operate more efficiently in the setting closer to their own nature and preference. This condition has now reached a point where

Sisters have been "invited" to teach in all-boys central high schools because priests and Brothers are not available. If and when such a practice persists over a period of time and a sufficiently broad scope of territory, Congregations will eventually reach the point of diminishing returns. Perhaps the decreasing ratio of religious women to men may be symptomatic of a decline already setting in. If then there be a lack of religious vocations to Congregations of Sisters, might not the relative productivity of different kinds of high schools, whether single-sex or coeducational, also be a factor.

The present study hoped to elucidate this point by determining the status of all-girls and coeducational high schools in nurturing vocations of religious women. These findings would clarify the future for recruitment and for secondary personnel placement, and at the same time underscore one of the chief reasons for vocation deficits at the present time.

Purpose and Scope of the Study

The research was designed to derive comparative data concerning the potential value or effectiveness of Catholic secondary schools for developing vocations. Comparisons were made between single-sex and coeducational schools to assess their relative value as sources of religious vocations. Conjoined to this fundamental aim were several subsidiary purposes: (a) to re-appraise current personnel practices in Catholic secondary schools as these have a bearing on the recruitment of vocations to the religious life; (b) to determine the factors associated with more effective provisions for vocations, and the extent to which characteristics of single-sex and coeducational high schools influence these factors; (c) to evoke from questionnaire responses a teacher-personality pattern most conducive to the development of vocations; and (d) to weigh recommendations from the questionnaire for the solutions to these problems.

The following sub-problems were related to the major area of investigation and were the foci of appraisal and analysis:

1. To what extent do the two major types of Catholic high schools and their subdivisions contribute to the vocation needs of the Catholic educational system?

2. To what extent is size of school related to the number of religious vocations?

3. Is teacher personality related to the number of students attracted to the religious life? What intangibles operate to enhance or destroy the ideal "teacher image" of dedicated professional competence in secondary education?

4. What is the thinking of Catholic high school teachers and administrators with regard to contemporary issues in secondary education, with special emphasis on the psychological aspects of single-sex versus coeducational systems?

5. Do priests, Brothers, and Sisters agree or differ in opinion with respect to coeducation as a policy for Catholic high schools in the United States?

6. What measures can be recommended for the solution of identified problems in vocation recruitment?

The core of the investigation centered around the statistical analysis of an actual vocation count evolving from a selected number of single-sex and coeducational Catholic high schools from 1954 to 1959. A large portion of the study, however, was concerned with the judgments and suggestions of high school teachers and administrators regarding related psychological aspects in the development of religious vocations.

LIMITATIONS OF THE STUDY

Nature of the Study. The survey approach of the present study necessarily emphasized the natural and prescinded from all the supernatural aspects of religious vocations. Emphasis rested on the psychological implications of the single-sex and coeducational classroom climates. The investigation sought only to compare and analyze the vocation response in the psychologically divergent atmosphere of these two climates. All other phases of the religious-vocation problem remained outside the scope of the present study.

Instrument. The questionnaire used was constructed according to the criteria advocated by experts in the field (Good & Scates, 1954). After careful formulation of its several component parts, the first draft was submitted to members of the Department of Psychology of the School of Education of St. John's University, and to a seminar of graduate students. On the basis of their suggestions, some sections were omitted as being irrelevant to the thesis. Other parts, including the title, were rephrased and a change of structure was adopted that would facilitate statistical analysis. With these suggestions incorporated in a revised form, the questionnaire was then used in a pilot study among administrative personnel similar to the participating population. Changes and recommendations of this trial group were included in the final printed form. A waiver of signature was offered to solicit frankness and sincerity in the judgments and opinions given.

The questionnaire consisted of eight printed pages and was divided into three parts. Part I gathered personal data from the respondents in a combination completion and checklist form, and touched on experiences related to their own vocations. Information issuing from this section served as a basis for comparison with the youth of today in the same area. Part II was designed to elicit opinions and judgments concerning certain aspects of secondary education, with emphasis on single-sex versus coeducational systems. The statements used contained implications for the development of religious vocations in Catholic secondary schools. Opinions were checked under the following symbols:

A—Complete agreement with the statement

B—Strong inclination to agree but with reservations

C—Inclination to disagree rather than to agree

D—Strong disagreement

X—Not in a position to judge

Respondents were encouraged to add comments wherever they thought them justified. Part III assessed several relatively intangible factors affecting both teacher and student as they react to each other during the learning process, thus indirectly affecting vocation choice. Among the topics covered in Part III were: (a) factors contributing to the successful teaching of adolescents on the secondary level; (b) conditions that may have operated to cause strain in the classroom; (c) effective presentation of guidance areas and school subjects to mixed groups of boys and girls; (d) school-type preferences of respondents; and (e) an evaluation of the scholastic needs of secondary school students. The final section of the questionnaire was devoted to open-end questions relating to psychological and pedagogical involvements in single-sex and coeducational schools as they affect both teacher and student. Opportunity was provided for criticisms of the systems now in operation and suggestions for their improvement, together with a request for a personality portrait of the ideal teacher.

The questionnaire was mailed to 778 prospective participants. Returns from the first mailing amounted to 469 or 60.3 per cent. A follow-up increased the percentage to 76.5. Although unanimous response to a questionnaire survey remains a researcher's Utopia, the more modest achievement of a 76.5 per cent return from the original sample provided a basis adequate enough for valid generalizations on the sample in question. Less than a full count of response tends to limit a study but does not negate its usefulness as a research instrument.

Even though popular from the researcher's point of view, the questionnaire as an inquiry instrument labors under the onus of several inadequacies: incompleteness, indefiniteness, and unreliability. A definitive interpretation of results cannot be expected under such conditions. However, the exigencies of time, place, and circumstance often necessitate the use of this research device in order to reach a widely scattered and varied population.

Population. Another factor limiting conclusions in this study was the population. The preliminary survey was sent to 200 independent motherhouses representing 100 teaching Congregations of Sisters in the United States, excluding Alaska and Hawaii. Major superiors in 142 motherhouses responded with data on their novitiates and sources of origin of their vocations. From this sample, a list of approximately 800 Sister teachers and administrators in Catholic secondary schools was derived and questionnaires mailed to them. A limited sampling of priests and Brothers was included also for comparative purposes.

Survey of Related Literature

The amalgam of factors which constitutes what is ordinarily considered a religious vocation can be dichotomized into two major elements, the natural and the supernatural. Any consideration of the supernatural aspects of religious vocations is as much outside the scope of the present study as an analysis of mental functions is beyond the periphery of surgery.

In conducting the survey of related literature, the investigator sought to evaluate the relative importance of many natural external factors on which religious vocations depend. Survey studies bearing on environmental relationships operating in this area would be relevant. Since environment is a comprehensive term variously defined, only studies of environmental relationships and religious vocations as these obtain in the general cultural milieu are included, particularly environment in the Catholic secondary school, whether rural or urban, single-sex or coeducational. Other tangential studies are cited merely to strengthen the thesis that a relationship between the number of vocations and type of school *does* exist and has repercussions in the various houses of formation in religious Congregations.

A research by Ziegler (1958) ascertained the environmental effects of both the single-sex and the coeducational types of schools on the personality, values, and adjustments of their student populations. The investigator stated that since environment exercised such a tremendous molding power on the adolescent, education must provide a school climate best calculated to produce the most acceptable personality patterns.

Subjects of the study were at the eleventh-grade level, 200 adolescent girls attending all-girls academies and 200 in attendance at parochial coeducational high schools.

Materials employed in this research included:

(a) Otis Quick-Scoring Mental Ability Test, Gamma Form Fm

(b) The California Test of Personality, Secondary Series, Form AA, 1953 revision

(c) The Allport-Vernon Study of Values, revised edition

(d) A Problem Check List

The Problem Check List was designed by the author to facilitate identification of problems in these six areas:

(a) home and family problems

(b) moral and religious problems

(c) health and personal problems

(d) social problems

(e) school problems

(f) vocational problems

In Ziegler's study of the values of high school girls, analysis of the data was confined to patterns of values. Comparisons were made between groups of means and between the groups' rank ordering of the six Allport-Vernon value areas. The three most prominent values for both groups were those in the religious, social, and political areas. Chi-square technique was applied to determine whether or not a real relationship existed between patterns of values and the group of which the subject was a member. The resulting chi-square value was found to be 14.132, which, with five degrees of freedom, was considered significant at the .02 level of confidence. Thus Ziegler concluded that there was demonstrated a tendency for girls attending all-girls academies and for girls attending coeducational parochial high schools to exhibit a pattern of values peculiar to their specific group.

Although the majority in both groups selected the religious as the highest evaluative attitude, value patterns in other areas of the Allport-Vernon Study of Values were significantly different, indicating that school environment may be a force in that direction. Since a sense of values is often the deciding factor in the choice of one's life work, the study pointed a tentative finger at school environment as a possible ingredient in the complex of factors operating in the genesis of a religious vocation.

Utilization of the critical ratio technique produced results that led to the conclusion that the two groups of girls attending two types of Catholic high schools were very much alike with respect to the number and kind of problems which they indicated in the Problem Check List. Of the six problem areas investigated, not one showed statistically significant differences. The present study sought to enlarge the scope of the Ziegler research by including diocesan high schools, both single-sex and coeducational. Rather than explore student attitudes, the investigator studied the problem from the teacher-administrator point of view.

Covering 7,500 subjects, one of the most thorough studies of vocations was made by Bowdern (1936). National in scope, Bowdern's study investigated the environmental influences affecting vocations to the priesthood and the religious life from 1919 to 1929. According to his findings, a vocation to the sisterhoods: (a) generally stemmed from a large family whose parents were practicing Catholics; (b) was frequently the product of a Catholic school (although the Catholic coeducational schools at the time of the Bowdern study contributed only a small proportion of vocations); (c) and had distinguishing intellectual as well as moral traits, since the majority of vocations came from the upper third of the class.

In the summary of impressions gathered from his questionnaire, Bowdern mentioned two observations which bear on the present study: (a) vocation-subjects did not attend coeducational high schools; (b) vocation-boys were taught by men, and vocation-girls were taught by women. Influenced by the suggestions of his respondents and his own findings, Bowdern offered some pertinent recommendations: the status of the religious Brother should be clarified; more Catholic high schools should be available; coeducation should be discouraged in the parochial system—at least separate classes should be maintained, if not separate buildings; and boys after sixth grade should be taught by men.

Barrett (1960) also studied the Catholic high school and the particular influence it exerts on religious vocational decision. Among the purposes of this study were: (a) To determine the Catholic high-school factors which definitely influence girls' vocation decisions; and (b) To investigate the stability of vocation decisions made during the high-school years. Barrett asked the 870 participants in the study to recommend the type of high school they considered best for a girl with a potential religious vocation. Their choices were as follows: 372, all-girls school; 233, coeducational school; 166, the community preparatory school; and 62, the co-institutional. Among her general conclusions, Barrett noted that "the greatest influence for or against religious life comes from the conduct, attitudes, and personality of the Sisters with whom the girls come in contact. It is the example of the religious teacher that helps most to bring potential religious vocations to fruition" (1960, p. 105). Barrett also recommended that high-school teaching Sisters double their efforts to attract young girls to the religious life by developing favorable teacher-student relationships, fostering interest "by friendliness rather than by subtle coercion."

A thorough coverage of vocation factors prevailing in the Cleveland and Youngstown dioceses was the objective of Hagan's study in 1944. By means of a questionnaire, Hagan gathered factual information on conditions and circumstances attending the call to the religious life. Respondents totaled 2,120 Sisters, representing 11 different Congregations with motherhouses in the dioceses studied. The classification of high schools according to types of administration was limited to parish, public, and convent schools. Respondents attributed their vocations to attendance at Catholic schools, relatives in religious life, spiritual guidance, and membership in religious organizations.

Beyond a factual report of the schools attended by the religious, Hagan attempted little interpretation of the data. The study revealed, however, that the median age for entrance to the religious life is 19 years, three months. This finding indicated that the high-school years were a ripe time for vocation fruition. The significance of the various schools in fostering vocations was shown in a summary. Grades six, seven, and eight surpassed any others in frequency of mention as the focal point for beginning thoughts on vocation. All four years of high school, not merely the upper two, were of about equal importance as periods of final decision. Because of the increased number and types of schools today, this analysis by Hagan was thought inadequate for a satisfactory interpretation of the present situation.

Garesché (1942) investigated conditions favorable to vocation growth by submitting questionnaires to Mothers General and Provincial of selected Congregations of religious women engaged in nursing, teaching, and mission work in the United States. In many cases, replies duplicated the findings of the Bowdern study made six years earlier. Noted as of special significance was the influence of a changing economy and political schema. Disillusionment, the threat of Communism, increased clerical interest in vocations, and Catholic environment during vacation ranked high as inducements toward religious life.

Elsewhere, Garesché (1950) observed that the current great demand for religious vocations to the sisterhoods was not a reproach to young women or to the religious Congregations of women. At present, almost three times as many girls enter the service of the Church as compared with boys who become priests or religious. Reasons for the shortage of religious women, as adduced by Garesché, might be summarized under the following headings: (a) the services of the Sisters are more appreciated today than heretofore; consequently they receive many requests to undertake new apostolic ventures; (b) mission needs are expanding; and (c) the number of religious Congregations has increased and so the pool of potential subjects is spread among more groups.

A previous study by Garesché (1941) sought causes for the relative dearth of vocations to the religious life of women. Garesché had sent a personal letter to a list of major superiors with a few questions whose combined answers would, he hoped, give a fair idea of the actual situation. Forty-three reports were used as the basis of his study. One question asked for the number of postulants who entered each responding community from 1936 to 1939. The combined totals for the 43 communities were as follows: 1936 - 951; 1937 - 905; 1938 - 882; 1939 - 855. Superiors judged they would need 1,203 postulants per year to maintain present personnel and allow for expansion. The estimate was about 27 per cent more than were applying at the time.

Garesché also asked for an enumeration of aids to the development of vocations. Listed in order were the following: (a) the influence of a good Catholic home; (b) love of the missions; (c) good literature; (d) the influence of the religious themselves; (e) school influence, especially the harmonious cooperation of the high-school faculty; and (f) the zeal of the clergy in promoting religious vocations.

Among the obstacles listed were: (a) the highly materialistic ambitions of parents for their children; (b) the spirit of selfishness in the homes; (c) a false sense of values; (d) the powerful appeal of present-day welfare work; (e) the wage-earning capacities of the modern girl; (f) delay in entering novitiates immediately after high-school graduation; (g) influence of non-Catholic colleges and public high schools; and (h) hindrances in the parochial school. The last obstacle was enlarged upon to include the points that follow. Education in the Catholic secondary school system, according to these respondents, unduly emphasized preparation for a professional or business career. Too much social activity enervated the students for the more serious program of intellectual development. Faculty and administration stressed intellectual rather than moral growth. Schools were becoming so large that "the conditions bring about an estrangement between the teachers and the students, and prevent that cordial and personal interest in the pupil which is so helpful and inspiring" (Garesché, 1941, p. 107).

Keenan's study (1953) also supported the view that environment appreciably affects religious vocations. By means of personal communications with Sisters, Keenan investigated the effects of cultural background on religious vocations among women. The study revealed that the optimum age bracket for vocations is 15-20. At this time, natural idealism, together with an awakening sense of responsibility and an urge to co-operate in the betterment of society, propels toward the goal of religious life. The summary of Keenan's findings indicated that: (a) parents must offset, with concern for larger values, the increased bonds of natural affection existing within the framework of the modern smaller family; (b) the concept of vocation needs further elaboration in school; and (c) the influence of materialism should not be discounted.

Keenan intimated that larger issues are sometimes superseded by apparently trifling considerations. These latter, however, rate high in the minds of youth, whose response to cultural pressure is apt to oppose higher evaluative considerations. As Keenan observed:

The natural basis of recruiting candidates for religious Orders will, perhaps, have to take account of the changed status of womanhood. Everyone knows that public status and the nun's habit are of secondary importance, as also the niche in the Catholic Directory and the strange names imposed on nuns, but these things appear to have a greater significance in the minds of youth than for those who are mature. It is youth, however, which will say yes or no (1953, p. 7).

Keenan also cited an investigation undertaken in 1944 by the Archdiocese of Chicago to discover the age group in which

vocations were most common among girls. Four thousand
Sisters gave the following information: nine per cent decided
at 12; 31 per cent, between 13 and 15; 44 per cent, between 16
and 20; and 16 per cent after 20. The biggest single fear of
subjects was that of making a wrong choice. The major obstacle for this group was the lack of guidance.

A study which highlighted the pivotal position of home
environment in stimulating vocation responses was made by
Garland (1951). Her findings revealed that domestic factors
like family recreations and family customs were potent in this
regard. Garland sent questionnaires to religious communities
in various parts of the United States and to 13 central high
schools for girls. Usable replies came from 156 Sisters, who
indicated factors which helped them decide to follow a religious
vocation. These data supported the hypothesis that a definite
relationship existed between vocations and home influence.

From the second group of participants in the Garland
study, namely, senior high school girls, 310 usable questionnaires were received. Data from these returns revealed: (a)
a marked increase in the number of smaller-sized families;
(b) a notable consequent decrease in vocations; (c) strong
parental objections to their daughters' entering religious life;
(d) a surprisingly large number of possible vocations in high
school senior classes at the time of the study; and (e) a large
number of girls who had at one time or another thought seri-
ously of entering the convent. Garland concluded that in great
measure the present lack of vocations can be traced to the fail-
ure of parents to have the "exceptional family" from which
vocations normally come and to the neglect of counselors to
encourage those who have at one time expressed their willingness to consider the religious life.

In the same vein, John and Eileen Farrell (1952), leaders
in the Cana Movement, pointed to the deteriorating influences
of the "twenties" and the "thirties" upon family life and marriage as probable causes for the slack today. They maintained
that the solution for this deficit rested with the promotion of
sound Christian family life.

Mulloy (1951) confirmed the conclusions of the Garland study with his research showing that most religious vocations come from a rich, deep family life. Vocations are in direct proportion to the solidity of Christian family living. According to the statistics offered by Mulloy, the Catholic population in 1950 was 3.18 times as great as in 1900, whereas the number of vocations was 3.53 times as numerous as in 1900. By 1950, the number of Brothers more than doubled; the number of priests almost tripled; and professed Sisters quadrupled the 1900 statistics in *The Official Catholic Directory*. Other comparative data cited by Mulloy showed one vocation for every 161 Catholics in 1900; one out of every 145 Catholics in 1950. In 1900, .6 per cent followed religious vocations; in 1950, .7 per cent. Although the difference of .1 per cent is numerically insignificant, when transformed into raw data, it spells out 20,000 more vocations.

To find a relationship between size of family and number of vocations, a study originating in Marygrove College, Detroit, and undertaken by Sister M. Christina (1941) tested the following hypothesis: "Since it is harder for children of the small family to get free of responsibility in order to dedicate themselves to God, then we may expect to find a close relationship between size of family and number of vocations."

The population of the study included students in a girls' college, juniors and seniors in seven parochial high schools whose families represented different social and economic strata, and students from one girls' central high school. All were located in a large industrial area. Seventy per cent returns to the questionnaire used in the study yielded the following data: (a) 227 vocations originated in the group of 1,135 respondents; (b) six of these 227 vocations came from the 1-3 family group; 91, from the 4-7 family group; and 130, from families with seven or more children; (c) 161 of the 227 were nuns, or 2.4 women to one man in religious life.

According to a summary of the data gathered in the Marygrove questionnaire, the research confirmed Garesché's findings of a disproportion between the present and previous generations in the ratio of boys' and girls' vocations, with the girls still in the lead although showing a definite decrease. For the Church as a whole, the ratio of women to men in religious life stood at 3:1; for the older generation, the parents of the respondents, the ratio was 3.3:1; for the children's generation, 1.1:1.

As a sequel to her research, Sister M. Christina (1942) questioned 1,700 Sisters from widely scattered communities in the United States in an effort to determine the ideal "vocation family." The age range of the subjects surveyed extended from 18 to 70 years. Half were born in large cities; about one-fifth were born on farms. Their economic status was average or lower middle class. Replies revealed that 81 per cent of the Sisters came from families of over four children and 11 per cent from families of three or fewer children. Further, the ratio of vocations for the general Catholic population in the United States was .9 per cent, greater than Mulloy's figures for 1950. The investigator noted that "one of the most important factors in fostering vocations, . . . is the interest, instruction, and encouragement of the boy or girl during adolescence" (Sister M. Christina, 1942, p. 13).

Among other findings, Sister M. Christina's study noted that 70 per cent of the Sisters decided their vocations between 13 and 19. Slightly fewer than 20 per cent decided after 19; a few, earlier than 13. The most important age level for vocational decision was 16, with a close second at 17. Eight, almost nine, of every ten attended parochial schools for at least part of their education. This fact pointed to the great power of Catholic education in fostering religious vocations, at least until the present era.

To summarize the findings of Sister M. Christina's study as they pertain to the present investigation: (a) significant ages for decision were 16 to 17; (b) fifty per cent were novices at 20; and (c) the great majority were educated in parochial schools. Some twenty years prior to Sister Christina's study just reviewed, research with high-school students showed that the curve of interest in vocations began with a few cases at

12 years, took a definite upward swing at 15, reached a peak at 16, and dropped suddenly away at 17 and 18. These age trends were reconfirmed in Sister Christina's investigation.

Concerning the general pattern of vocation interests during adolescence, the results of a study by McMahon (1957) may be cited. Ninety-four per cent of the subjects of this study, 600 girls in a diocesan girls' high school in New York City, admitted in reply to a questionnaire that they had contemplated the religious state and had thought of it as a personal way of life. In the same study, 65 per cent of the seniors one month before graduation continued to think of it "sometimes." Both findings substantiated the data of the Garland study as to the large number of possible vocations in senior classes and the high percentage of girls who had given religious life serious consideration. A profitable area of research might be to probe reasons for the discrepancy between the idealistic appeal of religious life and the lack of motivation to realize the ideal, as evidenced in McMahon's study.

An investigation by Evans (1951) delved into the problem of the origins of vocations to the teaching brotherhoods. Principal material for this study was obtained through questionnaires sent to 360 teaching Brothers. Evans also used selected responses on 380 applications for admisssion to the novitiate. Based on the population sample, general conclusions from the analysis of the data were as follows: (a) the desire to become a Brother usually originates where a boy can observe a Brother in action; (b) vocation thinking begins most frequently somewhere in the upper elementary grades; (c) about 40 per cent who eventually become Brothers find obstacles at the outset; and (d) the majority of obstacles are in the form of objections from those upon whose opinion the young aspirant relies.

Another study just completed by Coleman (1960) approached more directly the specificity of the present research. Coleman analyzed the effect of boy-girl relations on interest in and development of vocations among boys in boy-girl high schools and in all-boys high schools for the period 1954-1959.

The population for the study was drawn from 30 Catholic high schools in California, the majority from the Archdioceses of San Francisco and Los Angeles, with one sample from the Diocese of Sacramento and two samples from the Diocese of Monterey-Fresno.

Statistics based on Coleman's study indicated no appreciable difference between the two types of schools as sources of vocations to seminaries and novitiates. The researcher, however, found significant differences among the three kinds of boy-girl schools: coeducational, co-institutional, and co-instructional. The percentages of vocations to the average enrollment for each type of school included in the survey were as follows: all-boys, 4.2 per cent; boy-girl, 3.7 per cent. A finer discrimination among boy-girl types resulted in this analysis: coeducational, 3.9 per cent; co-instructional, 2.8 per cent; and co-institutional, 4.2 per cent. Although Coleman claimed no appreciable difference between the two major types, when prorated on the basis of a 100,000 boy-student population, the data become more meaningful: all-boys schools would have a vocation yield of 4,110 per 100,000 students for one year; boy-girl schools, 3,508 per 100,000 boy students for the same period of time.

A consistent trend in Coleman's research revealed boys more girl-conscious in all-boys schools than in the boy-girl situation. This facet of the study evolved from a questionnaire directed to 3,404 seniors who participated in the project. The survey accordingly cautioned against generalizations about the boy-girl relations factor as a deterrent for vocations to the priesthood or the brotherhood in boy-girl schools.

The present study, while it investigated the same general problem which served as the basis for Coleman's research, differed in scope, population sample, and types of schools involved. It drew its teaching and administrative population sample from 328 schools across the nation. The school types included those of the Coleman study, without making a separate category of the co-instructional school which, for the purpose of the present thesis, does not function differently from the co-institutional school, except in the area of the principal-ship. While Coleman investigated the problem from the "boy" angle, the present researcher evaluated factors as they related to adolescent girls and in consequence to the supply of novices in the formation centers of the various sisterhoods.

With a clearcut orientation toward secondary education, Shocklee (1957) investigated 83 coeducational high schools in 25 states. The enrollment ranged from 300 to over 2,000 students. The status of these 83 schools in relation to vocations was analyzed in detail. Most of their administrators were contacted. Shocklee's study showed that three per cent of the pupils enrolled entered seminaries or novitiates while in high school or after graduation. The larger schools had slightly higher percentages. Twenty-seven of the 83 had better than Shocklee's average representation in seminaries and novitiates among their students and graduates.

The administrators volunteered information about the difficulties of promoting religious vocations in coeducational high schools. One of the main obstacles to religious vocations in coeducation, according to the informants, involved the problem of "going steady," which, however, is not limited to boy-girl schools. While the main objection to coeducational schools in their relation to the vocation situation seems to be the proximity of boys and girls in the classroom, most administrators felt that this nearness had little or no effect on religious vocations. Schools participating in Shocklee's study were of comparatively recent origin. Forty-three of the 83 were begun after World War II; 30 were established since 1950.

A piece of research even more closely related to the current enterprise was a ten-year comparative study of the number and percentages of vocations to one Congregation of teaching Sisters in the Midwest from all-girls and coeducational high schools from 1949 to 1958, as reported by Sister Mary Teresa Francis (1960). All data were obtained from community archival records. Of the 755 persons involved in the study, 577 or 78 per cent of the novitiate personnel were graduates of all-girls schools; moreover, 463 candidates or 61 per cent of the total were graduates of all-girls schools taught by the community in question. In comparison, 178 or 24 per cent of the total came from coeducational schools. Of the 178, 94 or 12 per cent were educated in coeducational high schools taught by the community conducting the study, while only two per cent were from schools taught by other communities. According to the investigator, this finding would seem to indicate that girls are strongly attracted to the Sisters they know best, which emphasizes the human-relations factor involved in the issue and the strategic importance of classroom climate and school environment in the fostering and fruition of religious vocations.

For this community, the study revealed fluctuations in the number of vocations from year to year during the ten years under scrutiny, for all types of schools, and for each of the two major classifications also.

All types : Range—58 to 102 per year

All-girls : Range—46 to 81 per year

Coeducational : Range—2 to 21 per year

The small number of applicants from the 30 coeducational high schools throughout the United States in which these Sisters teach is, in the opinion of the research analyst, a matter of concern. This concern is duplicated throughout the country when major superiors compare the large part of their teaching personnel which is absorbed by the coeducational high school and the small returns in terms of religious vocations coming from the students enrolled in these schools.

In the same study of Sister Mary Teresa Francis, the participating group of 755 was analyzed for the number and percentage of candidates entering from schools of different sizes. Results showed that the smallest number of vocations from the all-girls schools taught by these Sisters came from the smallest schools during the ten-year period; 35 entered from small schools; 148 from the medium-sized schools; and 280 from the large schools. Data from the coeducational schools revealed a different pattern. More candidates entered from small coeducational schools; fewer from the medium-sized schools; and least from the large schools; respectively, 46, 32, and 16.

Percentages computed on the ratio of candidates from individual schools to number of graduates from these schools formed a basis for more valid comparison, since this procedure considered the variable of school enrollment. The resultant data clarified the status of the several school types in this respect and showed the vocation trends in each. In the all-girls schools, the percentages ranged as follows: 5.11 per cent, 5.18 per cent, and 3.64 per cent for small, medium-sized, and large schools respectively. In the coeducational schools, the results were: 2.18 per cent, 1.47 per cent, and .62 per cent for small, medium-sized, and large schools respectively.

The research reflected a national trend in the schools taught by the Congregation in question. The small coeducational parish high schools were disappearing and were being replaced by larger central coeducational high schools. Seven of the 17 small parish high schools taught by these Sisters had been converted during the past ten years; three more were due for the same change within the next two or three years. Implications for the future Sister-teacher supply are dark if present trends are fortified through the multiplication of the school type least calculated to nurture religious vocations; namely, the large diocesan coeducational plants.

Sister Mary Teresa Francis suggested that further study be made of the number of vocations to the priesthood and to the religious life for boys as well as girls, to compare the number and percentage of graduates who enter the seminary and the religious life from all-girls, all-boys, and coeducational schools. This has been done in part for the boys by the Coleman study and for the girls by the present research. A further suggested study would revolve about the significant differences in number and percentages of vocations from the several types of boy-girl schools: coeducational, co-institutional, and co-instructional. Such a study at the present time would be somewhat premature, since the fluid state of Catholic secondary school administration does not provide the stability conducive to reliable data. It had been previously planned to include co-institutional high schools as a separate category in this report for purposes of comparison, but returns revealed such ambiguity in the data, so many schools of this type functioning for less than five years, some in process of change to co-instructional, and others uncertain of their status, that this phase of the research was abandoned.

Several surveys have been prepared on the rural-urban factor in religious vocations. Will (1953) demonstrated that of the 417 Sisters teaching in the elementary schools of the Springfield, Illinois diocese during the year 1952-1953, 216 Sisters or 52 per cent were reared in cities and 201 or 48 per cent in rural areas. The national urban-rural ratio obtained by Bowdern for the years 1919-1929 revealed that 55 per cent of the vocations to the sisterhoods originated in urban areas and 45 per cent in rural areas. The findings of the Will study closely paralleled the data supplied by Bowdern for 1919-1929.

A further investigation of the urban-rural factor by Thienel (1954) revealed data which disagreed with both the Bowdern and the Will findings. Thienel found rural areas more productive than urban. These rural-urban studies, however, were tangential to the present research and are cited merely to indicate an awareness on the part of trend analysts of the importance of environment in the development of religious vocations.

The field of adolescent sex differentials abounds with studies related to its various phases. That boys and girls react differently to different school environments was shown by a study (Lotz, 1951) which sought to verify this basic hypothesis: the type of school, single-sex or coeducational, one attends has an influence on the development of one's social and emotional adjustment. Lotz also probed various sub-problems: (a) Are there discernible social and emotional needs indicated by entering freshmen in either type of school? (b) Are differences in social and emotional adjustment reflected by the seniors of the two types of schools? (c) Are there any particular social and emotional adjustment patterns which are related to four years attendance at either type of school?

Subjects of this study were 240 academic high school students, composed of the following groups: 30 freshmen and 30 seniors from an all-male school; 30 freshmen and 30 seniors from an all-female high school; and 60 freshmen and 60 seniors from a coeducational high school. The subjects were further equated on the basis of economic status, health, mental ability, and race. Tools for the inquiry were a differential battery of personality tests: (a) Rohde-Hildreth Sentence Completions, (b) Mooney Problem Check List, and (c) Bell Adjustment Inventory. Significant relationships were tested by these statistical techniques: the *t* test of significance, the chi-square test, correlation analysis, and Fisher's *z* function. Pertinent to the present investigation is that part of the conclusion which holds that ". . . according to this investigation, with its delimitations and as measured by the differentiating test battery, the coeducational school apparently has a significant relationship to the emotional and social adjustment of only the female adolescent" (Lotz, 1951, p. 63). All students, with the exception of coed female freshmen, believe that the single-sex school provides fewer distractions while at school.

Considerations of time and space warranted the decision not to include more of these studies in the review of related literature, since the narrow limits of a dissertation would prevent adequate treatment. Completeness of coverage, however, would indicate at least a glance at Knoebber's study (1933), which disclosed the attitudes and problems of 3,000 adolescent girls drawn from 30 public and private schools in the United States. Vocational problems of these girls assumed a position of first rank among those which usually plague the adolescent. The author summarized her findings in this regard as follows:

This [need for guidance] occurs in more tables and is mentioned by the girls with more frequency than any other single item. . . . Illustrations might be multiplied indefinitely to prove that girls of adolescent age begin to think with seriousness of their future and what it has in store for them (Knoebber, 1933, p. 171).

Fleege (1945) made a parallel investigation on the self-revelation of the adolescent boy. Because the current research was oriented toward Sister teachers and the adolescent girl, together with the implications of their mutual relationship for vocation output, Fleege's study was not particularly relevant.

Most of the studies included in this survey of related literature omitted statistical analysis beyond a casual nod to the arithmetic mean. From available information it would seem that the investigation in hand is the first attempt at a more discriminating analysis of data bearing on feminine reaction to classroom climate in Catholic secondary schools as related to vocation response. The chi-square test and *rho* correlations were the two principal statistical devices used to interpret the impassive data gathered by the research instrument.

Significance of the Study

Reports from the U. S. Office of Education on the current school year emphasized the need for an enlarged teacher corps. National school and college enrollments increased this academic year for the fifteenth consecutive time, with an increment of 1,940,000 over last year. The total for the 1959-1960 term is 46,480,000. Of the 1,546,000 teachers needed to handle this total, only 1,360,000 are available, leaving a substantial deficit. These figures spell out the current critical need for teachers in the national school picture.

Parochial and private schools throughout the country also wrestle with the teacher-personnel problem. For the purposes of the thesis only statistics referring to Sister teachers and the Catholic secondary school system were used in this section. Mangini (1958) reported that the percentage increase of secondary school students over 1950 was 34.45 per cent for 1957. National Sister teacher increase was 14.59 per cent. Even including lay teachers, the total faculty percentage increase in

Sisters' schools was 22.57 per cent, still far behind student percentage increases. This teacher shortage among Sisters is related to the vocation shortage, a matter of concern to religious communities and the hierarchy alike.

National trends in Sisters' secondary schools by types, 1950-1956, clearly indicated a swing toward diocesan secondary schools (Mangini, 1958). Average rate of increase:

Private secondary: .40 per cent per year

Parochial secondary: -1.70 per cent per year

Diocesan secondary: 9.24 per cent per year

It is in the secondary schools, whether single-sex or co-educational, that student distribution by sex and the attendant psychological complications become relevant to the nurture of vocations to the religious life. Through the present study, statistical returns from high schools in the United States revealed which of the various types are accompanied by the greatest percentages of religious vocations.

As suggested in the Mangini study, profitable research might be conducted to determine the connection between school types and problems in Sister-teacher personnel placement. This constituted one facet of the present research. As worded in Mangini's study, the problem of Sister-teacher placement is embodied in this question: "Because of their limited numbers, where can the Sisters use their influence most thriftily for the good of this generation of youth for whom they share the responsibility?"

A . . . problem facing Sister teachers in administrative positions is that of an equitable distribution of Sister teacher personnel through the various areas of Catholic education and also among the degree fields in higher education. . . . the proportion of Sister teachers is overly large [on the elementary level] whereas the lay teacher ratio is less than might be expected. . . . If the present proportion of Sisters to lay teachers in elementary schools is retained, and if 75 per cent of the Sister teachers continue to enter elementary schools, there will be a swift and progressive decrease of Sisters available for other areas of education. . . .

Survey figures have shown, too, that the rate of increase among Sisters in secondary schools is not so rapid as it needs to be in order to meet the teacher demand. . . . This is a serious loss because psychologists tell us that the high school student is probably the greatest potential of a given society. . . . One wonders what great good could be done if more well-trained Sister teachers and lay teachers were available for the secondary schools (Mangini, 1958, p. 256).

If the present study would show the superiority of the single-sex schools for religious vocations, community planners may well decide that a re-allocation of more Sisters to these secondary schools would be a wise concession to the needs of feminine psychology, both from the student's and the teacher's point of view.

Statement of the Hypotheses

The research was designed to test the following major hypothesis and three subsidiary hypotheses:

1. Because the coeducational system in high school influences girls during their most impressionable years, a relationship could be expected between type of high school and productivity in the area of religious vocations. The relationship might be expressed as follows: more girl-vocations come from all-girls schools than from coeducational schools.

2. Because of the psychological differences between the sexes, the most productive environment for religious vocations of the students is offered when teachers are of the same sex as their students.

3. Teacher respondents would prefer the teacher to be of the same sex as the pupil for vocation purposes.

4. One of the strongest influences in fostering vocations to the religious life is the personality of the religious teacher.

CHAPTER II

Related Phases of the Study

As human nature reproduces itself through marriage, so religious life, too, perpetuates itself under God through the instrumentality of human beings. Among these instrumental causes, the teacher's influence for good or ill is incalculable. Teacher personality is a potent factor in drawing youth to imitation. The contrary is also true—personality blemishes and character defects repel aspiring youth. For these reasons, the investigator sought a relationship among the various factors inherent in the situation today: the educator, the educand, classroom climate, and vocations. The atmosphere engendered for the adolescent by both teacher and peer group may be a subtle motivator or deterrent in affecting attitudes and reactions that may culminate in permanent value choices.

Rather than define the terms involved in the present study, a task fraught with semantic subtleties, the investigator chose to introduce the data analysis proper by discussing the implications for religious vocations of classroom climate in coeducational and single-sex situations, and adolescent sex differences as they relate to school life.

Religious Vocations

General Observations

In its widest as well as its narrowest sense, vocation rests on the knowledge of man provided by the disciplines of theology and psychology. Although psychology has earned a respectable berth on the roster of human knowledge, its penchant for standardized statistical procedures and its preoccupations with individual differences may annoy the uninitiated. Mailloux observes:

> To those who are fully aware of the amazing complexity of human conduct, this parallel evolution of two disciplines, which are struggling strenuously to grasp it in all its most significant dimensions . . . simply reveals,

27

once more, that our knowledge of man is still fragmentary, and that only the joint efforts of closely related disciplines, representing widely diversified methodological approaches, can justify our hope for the attainment of a synthesis, satisfying for our mind and illuminating for our action (1954, p. 63).

A religious vocation is a mystery. This view might justify a moratorium on attempts to explain the inexplicable, yet a mystery can be contemplated and a vast fund of intellectual enrichment garnered from the experience. Obviously, the scientific limitations of the present study prevent an exhaustive treatment of a topic that depletes human resources. Certain tangibles operate in the genesis of a religious vocation, however, and to give reassurance of their importance the investigator has touched lightly in the ensuing pages on certain so-called instrumental causes like school environment and concomitant factors.

Time Factor

Commenting on the age of onset of a religious vocation, Lochet (1956) indicates that very young children already have apostolic initiatives that are at least astonishing. He believes that a certain orientation of devotedness, an authentic sacerdotal or missionary vocation, can arise in the heart of a child. The formed and definitive vocational plan, however, matures during adolescence, between the ages of 13 and 17. Lochet calls adolescence the "age of the ideal, dreamed of and consented to." Significantly, Leclercq (1955) places the usual age for vocation during adolescence. In this period, Leclercq notes, a human being discovers the direction of his destiny at a time when he is most sensitive to spiritual values. If vocations may awaken in early childhood but a final choice is usual at puberty, then such natural concomitants of vocation like school environment and teacher-pupil-peer relationships assume greater importance.

Environmental Factors

Environment in general is a composite of many interrelating forces, the sum total of all the stimuli impinging on an individual from conception until death. From an objective point of view, environment seems to offer identical opportunities within any particular ambit, yet each person is highly selective in his response to stimuli. For the adolescent, each choice is a function of previous environmental pressures and orientation. Under the vast cumulative effect of many such choices, the plastic adolescent personality is molded by whatever adult pattern the culture approves.

The most potent environmental influences stem from the person-to-person relationships that punctuate human living. The adolescent, prone to idealize the adults within the confines of his experience, finds in his environment the challenge of choice between the high road and the low. In this sense, religious vocations often owe their bud and bloom to the environmental stimulation of dedicated teachers and classmates. While the whole system of vocation recruitment is something quite new in our times, according to Blowick (1932), in its most elemental form it is the impact of a mature and noble personality upon the susceptibilities of the adolescent. Viewed from this angle, it is only a throwback to the technique of Christ Himself, Whose "Come, follow Me" set in motion the recruiting program of religious vocations throughout the ages. Leclercq's words echo this invitation of Christ and point to a new concrete setting for its announcement:

> . . . God does not work except through the medium of men, and as soon as a man of God appears, vocations arise in his footsteps, truly authentic vocations, though awakened by him . . . [for] a man undergoes the influence of his surroundings. Vocations are even bound up with, not only the religious man or the religious institution which has opened the mind to supernatural realities, but with everything in education. Certain surroundings do not produce vocations, others produce them in abundance; certain surroundings only produce good

ones, others produce plenty that are mediocre (1955, p. 55).

The present study explored the implications of Leclercq's thought by assessing the relative merits of several types of school environment as these relate to the production of vocations.

Among contemporary scholars, Edith Stein ranks high as a keen and perceptive thinker. This disciple of Husserl and and later Carmelite contemplative met the mystery of her vocation in its culmination in the gas chambers of Auschwitz. Prior to her tragic end, Edith Stein formulated a theory of vocation which merits study. Especially does she credit with importance the meetings, casual or otherwise, that dot man's daily life, thus lending support to the writer's view that social relationships evolving through the learning process are of the utmost significance.

> The calls which progressively develop our vocations make themselves known to our souls through the mediation of various persons we meet on our way. . . . The "mystery of personal encounters," as Gabriel Marcel calls it, can be grasped only by those who see a meaning in every meeting and assess it as a divinely-given sign (Devaux, 1958, p. 173).

Studies of environmental influences on religious vocations are almost unanimously agreed concerning the prime importance of environment in this respect. To substantiate the premise that environment does play an appreciable role in the development and fruition of religious vocations, the investigator will cite studies already mentioned in the chapter on related literature, but which have particular relevance here. Garesché (1941), Garland (1951), Mulloy (1951), and Keenan (1953) found the influence of the home significant in the evolution of religious vocations, since vocations are in direct proportion to a deep Christian life. Masson (1958) investigated the influence of environment on vocations to the priesthood in the former Belgian Congo, Ruanda, and Urundi, and concluded that "the 'milieux of life' have a real importance, confirmed by figures, and amongst them the family (plus the school) has a select place." Masson's findings have been underscored through data from the present research which showed highly significant differences between all-girls schools and coeducational schools in the number of vocations to the sisterhoods coming from each. For a school on any level, especially the secondary, climate, atmosphere, and environment are vital in the formation of intellect and will, both functioning actively in the choice of a vocation.

Bowdern (1936), Garesché (1942), and Sister Mary Teresa Francis (1960) also testified to the place of the school in the development of religious vocations. The latter's ten-year study of coeducational and single-sex high schools staffed by her community revealed that the single-sex schools were more productive of religious vocations than the coeducational schools. In fact, the meager success of the coeducational schools in this respect warranted serious consideration by planning and administrative boards to obviate possible miscalculations in provisions for the future. Previous to the study of Sister Mary Teresa Francis, Bowdern (1936) also found that his vocation-subjects, by and large, were not the products of coeducation. Garesché's study (1942) did not specify areas or systems of superior worth, but merely indicated that school influence was important.

A religious vocation, all other things being equal, stems from value choices that are the outgrowths of attitudes emerging from referential frameworks. The initial stage in attitude formation consists in judgments based on perceptions and evaluations. When the frame of reference is a materialistic culture, dominated by sense values, obviously only strong countercurrents of thought can turn the tide in favor of those spiritual values that are implied in a call to religious life. Should the school, under whatever pretext, reinforce this emphasis on the material, such a philosophy would leave its impress on the student's concept of values. Religious vocations do not flourish where undue emphasis rests on the pragmatic criterion of present utility and enjoyment, because this measure of value contravenes the supernatural norms of a true vocation. In this bipolarity of sentiment and ideal, the adolescent understand-ably yields to peer pressure, which is often strengthened by the standards of his school. Ward highlights the strategic im-portance of school climate when he says: "Certainly in the order of practical learnings, which means all the arts and the intellectual virtue called 'prudence', the atmosphere—Christian or pagan, Catholic or Communist—is decisive" (1958, p. 100).

To develop preferred and chosen patterns of behavior, to stimulate thinking with the Church and working for her in-terests, Catholic educators must prevent incompatible kinds of growth. A school educates effectively to the degree that its declared aims and actual deeds are unified, and tension between theory and practice reduced to a minimum. The Catholic sec-ondary school system might profitably re-examine its policy in adolescent education to probe the extent to which its activ-ities harmonize with its philosophy, especially with regard to the optimum conditions for developing in the adolescent a re-ceptive attitude toward a call to the religious life.

Conclusion

The investigator presumed to synthesize all that has been written on religious vocation, whether from the point of view of theology or psychology, by outlining its principle of causal-ity thus:

(a) Material cause: predisposing factors—necessary qualifications of body, mind, and heart.

(b) Formal cause: the will of God (divine invitation).

(c) Efficient cause: acceptance of the call by the person; acceptance of the person by the religious superior.

(d) Final cause: the glory of God and the salvation of souls.

(e) Instrumental cause: external factors—teachers, so-cial pressures, school environment, etc.

ADOLESCENT SEX DIFFERENCES

While the broad foundations of religious vocations were roughly outlined in the preceding section, two specific phases of the present study called for further clarification: (a) adolescent sex differences and their implications; and (b) school environment, with special consideration of coeducation.

The adolescent is embroiled in various cross- and countercurrents which flow from his personal endowments and his cultural matrix. Borrowing from Lewin's field theory, the investigator considered the adolescent as a unit comprising the ego and extra-ego environmental field of social relationships. Environment and existence are mutually necessitous terms. It is patent, therefore, that the adolescent does not move in a vacuum. In the following section, adolescent sex differences will be considered from a three-fold point of view: biological, cultural-social, and educational. School environment, as consolidating and intensifying these differences, will be treated in terms of its relationship to the adolescent and to religious vocation.

General Observations

Being male or female is nothing else than being human in one of the two basic modes under which being human occurs. But as Sheehan (1955) notes, sex conditions the whole person with masculine and feminine traits, without being limited to physiological actions and reactions. To deny the influence of sex and other biological factors on the human psyche is as unreasonable as to "deny the role which the elemental forces welling up from the interior of the earth exert on a tree or flower" (Winkler, 1960, p. 10).

Biological Aspects

A biological basis may underlie the disparate attitudes, interests, and personality traits of the growing boy or girl, Tyler (1956) suggests. Superiority in size, strength, and motor ability sets the pattern of energetic behavior for all males and contrasting action guides for all females. Terman (1946) asserts that these varying modes of behavior stem partly from gonadal factors, as evidenced by changes that accompany sexual maturation and by the personality deviations characteristic of hypogonadal conditions.

Emotion and temperament likewise have a biological basis. Hartmann (1934) advises that noteworthy sex differences must be sought in the emotional and temperamental aspects of life, in broad fundamentals like *Weltanschauung,* dispositions, sentiments, and value hierarchies. To explain why some objects or experiences should consistently appeal more strongly to women than to men, Hartmann concludes that "the various goods of life fuse into different intensity patterns, depending upon the nature of the organism in which they reside" (1934, p. 112). One of the most important factors affecting the hierarchy of values is the "biological cleavage" of sex.

Cultural-Social Aspects

While research substantiates the *fact* of these sex differences, neither psychology nor social anthropology agrees in pinpointing the cause. Physical differentiation, although basic and innate, is not the full, complete, and adequate explanation. Biology alone does not solve the problem. On the objective side, cultural demands mold the personality until conformity to a sex stereotype results. Whether a person is male or female *biologically* depends on genetic and biological processes; to be male or female *socially* and *psychologically* depends on learning, environment, and experience (Brown, 1956). Conformity to group *mores* often processes man into a rubber stamp of his cultural peers. Behavior patterns are governed in large measure by social learning conditions. Bernard (1957) attributes sex differences to dissimilar interests and activities rather than to biological predispositions. Differential treatment from birth is another causative factor, as fundamental for the understanding of the adolescent as is the earlier sexual maturation of girls. From the greater supervision and protection of girls and the position defined for them by sex and social standards emerges the more emotional type of female personality. Girls are "protected" from things about which they "ought to be" afraid (Kuhlen, 1952).

With each sex functioning as a kind of sub-culture in the contemporary historical scene, American society expects its boys and girls not to act in the same way. The family, as major training agent, teaches the child to conform to approved patterns of behavior, with a consequent production of constellations of personality traits typical of boys and girls. Marked differences, rooted in cultural coercion, exist between boys and girls in the accomplishment of certain specified developmental tasks (Schoeppe, 1953). These include: (a) learning an appropriate inner and outer sex role; (b) achieving inner and outer emotional independence of parents and other adults; (c) forming conscience, morality, and a sense of values; (d) socializing with peers; and (e) developing intellectual skills. Milner (1949) sees social expectation as crucial in the child's training toward its sex role, and considers it a far more dominant variable in the genesis of such differences than studies have thus far shown.

Adolescent physiological, intellectual, and emotional changes can be properly understood only in relation to cultural and social influences. Strang (1957) observes that the adolescent views himself, his world, and his future according to the varying degrees of influence exerted by many personal-environmental conditions. Accepting attitudes between and within sex groups in any particular classroom situation may be due to: (a) home socio-economic level; (b) extent of pleasant group associations; (c) adult attitudes toward sex differences (Bonney, 1954). These factors take precedence, it is believed, over constitutional differences as motivators for social acceptance or rejection. Terman (1946) also considers exposure to the countless subtle differences in social influences as a causative factor for the gulf between girls and boys. These varied pressures begin early and operate continuously. Terman lists areas dominated by such pressures: clothing, recreation, restriction of mobility, home and school discipline, parental associations, occupational experience, educational exposures, and innumerable ideals of conduct and life satisfactions. Harris (1959) notes that a changed cultural ethos effects changes in adolescent interests. His study, which sought to investigate divergent social trends between 1935 and 1957, revealed recent developments in social activity. Today young people tend to marry younger and to show earlier preoccupation with social relations, love, and marriage. Girls rather than boys manifest greater interest in personal attractiveness, love, marriage, mental health, philosophy, and beliefs; boys, in money, health, and recreation. Here the female propensity for spiritual values contrasts with the male preoccupation with the material.

Anthropological research emphasizes the role of cultural pressures in the development of sex stereotypes and in the vicissitudes of adolescence (Douvan, 1957; Mead, 1949). A European writer (Schröteler, 1942) also attributes sex differences to the masculine-orientated culture of the past thousands of years. Man's intellectual activity has been fathomed to a greater depth than his emotional and volitional life, which is woman's chief domain. Muscle and mind have been the male preserve for aeons, and this slowly dying culture pattern may cause the evident stresses and strains of adjustment between the sexes in whatever relates to their development and education. One eloquent phase of this adjustment process is the dialogue between the sexes in secondary education. Girls seem to be more susceptible to the psychological nuances of interpersonal relations than are boys, and thus their needs in this respect may demand a curriculum and an environment designed especially for them. Forcing the female personality into an administrative groove that fits the male may have many repercussions. Not the least of these may be evident in the relatively meager flow of vocations to the sisterhoods from coeducational schools. It is the purpose of the present study to supply pertinent data evolving from a nationwide sampling of single-sex and coeducational Catholic high schools.

Educational Aspects

Considerations thus far have been based on the biological and cultural differences between male and female. It might be opportune here to indicate sketchily a few differences which have implications for education. Basic to all data on adolescent sex differences is the fact that boys and girls, reaching puberty at different ages, manifest different patterns of sexual maturation, and have different problems. Because of coeducation and automatic promotion in the American school system, boys and girls reach junior high school together, just when the girls are beginning to mature. Cole states that "the period from ages 12 or 13 to ages 14 or 15 is the worst possible time for boys and girls to be educated together, because they are too dissimilar in their size, physiological age, interests, and attitudes" (1958, p. 87). Mead confirms this view somewhere with the facetious observation that the only association boys of junior high school age should have with girls of the same age bracket is to growl at them.

The earlier social maturation of the girl, together with her natural propensity for a greater sociality, makes high school life for her a series of personal adventures or misadventures as she tries to find her place in its dynamism. It is a common belief that one of the most deeply rooted feminine characteristics is an absorbing interest in persons and personal relationships (Terman, 1946). The most important and conspicuous consideration in a relationship is the emotion resulting from contact. If this be so, and if it be also true that girls are deeply aware of the subtleties involved in personal encounters, then the human-relations factor in the school situation, whether engendered by peers or teachers, has a decided effect on them. A girl's associations carry a higher emotional charge than the boy's. Hence, social environment may have a more decisive part to play in the decisions she makes concerning her life's goals.

Traditionally, girls have been credited with high academic achievement. Ford's study (1957) revealed a heavy preponderance of girls among over-achievers, perhaps because academic success has greater prestige value for girls than for boys. The latter seek to validate their maleness through appropriate behavior in other areas, since scholastic laurels rest uneasily on the male brow at puberty. Girls, however, lack alternatives, so they channel their energies into the academic field. This discourages male efforts by lending a feminine "taint"' to intellectual achievement. Milner (1949) found that girls are more apt to be motivated by cues of the classroom situation than boys. Her research confirms the data on over-achievement revealed by the Ford study. In the American culture, adolescent girls experience a change of emphasis concerning achievement (Mead, 1949). As they mature, it becomes increasingly evident to them that competition with the male is ultimately unrewarding because of cultural pressures which favor male domination. The female role begins to take shape as uncompetitive; the male role, almost exclusively that of achievement.

A survey of studies in motivation (Diserens & Vaughn, 1931) contains two pertinent to the present purpose. Usnadze (1942) evaluated the opinions of 660 boys and 950 girls, ages 10-15, on motives of preference in school studies. Boys, he found, appreciated studies for intellectual and practical reasons; girls were motivated by emotional considerations. Punishment as a kind of motivation was investigated by Droege (1926), who asked 1,400 children, 8-14 years of age, to evaluate the punishments used in school work. According to his report, boys stressed the immediate, physical, practical effects; girls accentuated the remote, aesthetic, social consequences. Millar (1949) points to mental and emotional differences involved in learning:

A woman may become a very distinguished Latin scholar, but she does learn Latin in a different way from her brother. Certainly, if she has the capacity for classical studies, equity demands that she should have every opportunity in following the classical curriculum. But the best result would not be obtained if she is taught by a man along with a class of boys (1949, p. 79).

According to Terman (1946), boys expressed preferences for school subjects in the following order: science, mathematics, history, English, and languages. Girls ranked their choices in this order: English, commercial studies, languages, history, mathematics, and science. However, the appeal of a subject to a given sex may be due to instructional methods, subject-matter content, teacher personality, and associations with the peer group in class.

Although priority in academic achievement is sacrosanct to the female, school marks may derive from a composite of influences: motivation, interest, and personal characteristics. In other words, they are a function of the total background of the student, not of native endowment alone. The fact that girls often get better marks may be due to a lack of individualization in academic evaluation and greater partiality to the more compliant traits of girls. Another factor may be noted. Since it is alleged that women teachers favor girls in marking, and since women teachers are in the majority, sex differences in school marks may be attributed to sex bias in this area, rather than to differences dependent on the intellectual caliber of the achiever.

Chen's study (1937) revealed that investigations from 1910 to 1933 are probably right in showing women inferior, in varying degrees, to men in problem-solving ability. This may be due to a lack of interest and insufficient motivation, rather than to defect in ability. After comparing test results of boys and girls in mixed classes taught by women, boys taught by men, and girls taught by women, Dale (1926) concluded that steady sex differences were not evident, only indications of the better development of reasoning power in the boys taught by men than in the girls taught by women.

Sex differences prevail throughout life in nature's arrangement for the species, but the period of adolescence is their heyday. These differences extend beyond their external manifestations to the inner sanctum of the personality. Here, too, a difference is manifest, for sex is closer to the core of the female personality. Its impulses and vagaries pervade her experiences to a greater extent than they do the male's. Hence, environmental situations that have a zero effect on the boy register with strong emphasis on the girl whose susceptibilities in this area are tender and all-pervasive. For this reason, coeducation during high school is for the maturing girl a prolific source of emotional tension. It brings into sharp relief her natural interest in the young male. It causes frustration in the academic field, since to win social approval where it counts most for her means to relinquish scholastic achievement. This is to be expected because the *mores* require it.

Houlahan's study (1951) suggested the need for a varied approach to the handling of high school boys and girls in the effort to assist them to develop desirable personalities. Emotional development, a vital ingredient in religious formation, differs in both. Their religious outlook does not follow the same pattern. The formation of ideals and modes of thought consonant with religious vocations is hampered for either sex when the lines of approach are geared to one or the other. Boys dictate the tempo of the class. When topics are calibrated on the scale of their interests and needs, those that would stimulate the girls usually settle to the bottom of the list.

Despite the traditional stand of the Church and the more recent pronouncements of the Holy See, complete segregation of the sexes is not a standard for Catholic high school education. All the advantages of coeducation in high school (and there are some) may be achieved by a well-coordinated program of co-recreation, a feature prominent in the co-institutional school (Spiers, 1951). Millar (1949) reminds us that the purposes of the Creator are served only when each sex develops along its own proper lines.

CHAPTER III

SUBJECTS, MATERIALS, AND PROCEDURES

The present investigation involved a comparison and an analysis of the effectiveness of several types of Catholic secondary schools in the United States in fostering vocations to the religious sisterhoods. It had for its primary purpose to investigate the relationship between patterns of administration and productivity of religious vocations. It aimed to answer the fundamental question whether the influence of school environment affected significantly the flow of religious vocations to the sisterhoods. Two basic categories of administration in this country are the single-sex and the coeducational, with further subdivisions into parish, central, and private for each group. The study proposed: (a) to compare the data submitted by Sister-educators in these schools with those presented by priests and Brothers in the same field; and (b) to determine the relationships among the data obtained from the participating groups. This chapter describes the subjects who participated in the investigation, the materials used, and the procedures employed in carrying out the study.

SUBJECTS

Since the primary interest of the research was to test an hypothesis relating to the religious sisterhoods, the bulk of the data would be sought from religious women. In April, 1960, a letter (Appendix A) requesting permission to canvass their respective communities was sent to 200 out of the 491 Mothers General and Provincial of the active congregations, as distinguished from those which are strictly contemplative. These major superiors represented the independent motherhouses of congregations in the United States engaged in the field of secondary education specifically. Together with the letter were two forms. One form (Appendix B) requested the names of prospective respondents to the questionnaire, chief instrument of the study. The questionnaire was designed to

41

elicit data relating to the number of religious vocations from the schools taught, either in whole or in part, by members of their communities. Since the major superiors chose the names of the respondents, personal bias on the part of the investigator was obviated.

The second form (Appendix C) sought information concerning types of high schools previously attended by members of each community, whether postulants, novices, or junior professed Sisters. Each of these groups has varying time limits in different communities. A time bracket of ten years for the combined groups in the total number of participating communities would be a safe range, accounting for six years as junior professed Sister until the time of perpetual vows, two years as novice, and one year as postulant. Some communities have another category called the candidacy, which lasts from six months to one year. The data were calculated to confirm what would be shown by the reporting high schools for the years 1954-1959. However, while the high schools produced data about entrance into *any* religious congregation of women, the motherhouses provided data on vocations to teaching sisterhoods specifically. The religious communities would thus also give evidence of the relative value of the single-sex and the coeducational systems in fostering religious vocations.

Of the 200 religious superiors contacted, 142 or 71 per cent indicated their willingness to cooperate by sending the requested vocation data and the lists of prospective respondents. From these lists of administrators and teachers in charge of their schools emerged the population of the present study, exclusive of the priests and Brothers who were included for comparative purposes. Table 1 shows the sampling as related to the total number of Catholic secondary schools in the United States. According to organizational patterns, the main categories are: parish, central, and private. In its General Summary, *The Official Catholic Directory* for 1960 lists 1567 high schools, without however distinguishing between parish and central. Because this distinction was necessary for the pur-

TABLE 1

POPULATION SAMPLE AND NATIONAL TOTALS OF CATHOLIC SECONDARY SCHOOLS

Description	Parish			Central			Private		
		A	B		A	B		A	B
Total no. of Catholic secondary schools (1960 Directory)	1100			467			866		
Total no. contacted	249			220			232		
% of national total	22.6			47.1			26.8		
No. of respondents	176	137 complete — A	39 partial — B	117	63 complete — A	54 partial — B	154	128 complete — A	26 partial — B
% of national total	16.0	12.5	3.5	25.1	13.5	11.6	17.8	14.8	3.0
% of total sample	70.7	55.0	15.7	53.2	28.6	24.6	66.4	55.2	11.2

poses of the research, the investigator surveyed the directory data for each diocese and noted the classifications of the schools. Under the general title of the *Catholic Directory* summary were included types as varied as the following: diocesan coeducational, diocesan co-institutional, diocesan co-instructional, parish co-institutional, parish co-instructional, and interparochial. Where the administration to all appearances functioned under the authority of the local parish unit, the school was considered a parish high school; if the administration appeared centralized either in the diocese or within the focus of several parishes, the school was considered diocesan or central. By thus reclassifying these 1,567 schools, the investigator could list them as 1,100 parish high schools and 467 central high schools. The Directory also listed 866 private high schools. It might be a distinct service to future researchers in this area to have the Directory listing more specific with regard to high school type, a matter understandably difficult at the present time because of the uncertain status of so many schools.

Questionnaires (Appendix D), together with a letter explaining the purpose of the study, were sent to: 249 parish high schools or 22.6 per cent of the national total; 220 central high schools or 47.1 per cent of the national total; and 232 private high schools or 26.8 per cent of the national total. Sister administrators and teachers in the parish high schools answered to the number of 176, or 70.7 per cent of the number contacted, 16.0 per cent of the national total. Central schools were represented by 117 respondents, or 53.2 per cent of the number contacted, 25.1 per cent of the national total for schools of this type. Private schools produced 154 respondents, or 66.4 per cent of the number contacted, 17.8 per cent of the national total for private high schools.

The returned questionnaires were divided into two main categories, Group A and Group B. Group A contained those responses that were complete with regard to the core data relating to the number of vocations to the priesthood, brotherhood, and sisterhood from 1954-1959. Some schools failed to supply this information for several reasons. Accordingly, when the final sorting and counting were completed, the relative strengths of the three main administrative types in the survey were as follows: 12.5 per cent of the national total of parish high schools, 13.5 per cent of the national total of central high schools, and 14.8 per cent of the national total of private schools. The percentages of types of schools were closely matched, according to the number of schools employed in this study.

Group B of the questionnaire responses contained those which were incomplete with regard to the main data on the number of vocations from the respective schools during the period 1954-1959. This group was combined with Group A for all other sections of the questionnaire analysis. The incompleteness of the data was due to several reasons: (a) lack of statistics on the number of vocations; (b) inaccessibility of the files; (c) recency of establishment (less than five years); and (d) unexplained reasons.

The first mailing of the questionnaire was directed to 778 administrators and teachers, of which number, 469 or 60.28 per cent responded. A follow-up procedure on inadvertent non-respondents raised the percentage to 76.48 or a total of 595 respondents. An attempt was made to discover the reasons for the non-response to the first contact. Of the 57 Sisters who cooperated with this phase of the inquiry, 11 gave the untimeliness of the approach as their reason, ten stated that they had never received the questionnaire, ten had mislaid it, nine thought it too long, eight were discouraged from answering it because of the pressure of other duties, four had insufficient data or experience to comply, and three pleaded illness. Only two of the group admitted that they had discarded it.

The 595 Sister respondents were classified as 447 administrators and 148 teachers. For comparative purposes, 33 priests and 40 Brothers engaged in full-time teaching or administration on the secondary level were included in the survey. Five of the 33 priests were invited through a personal interview to participate in the study. The remaining 28 were reached by mail. Their names were furnished by the major superiors of the teaching communities who were participating in the study. These religious superiors, in the 28 instances in question, had sent the names of priest-principals or priest-counselors as contact agents for the schools involved, rather than the names of their Sisters.

The Brothers responding resulted from the list of Brothers printed in *The 1960 Catholic Directory.* All congregations of Brothers engaged in teaching on the secondary level were invited to participate. Of the eight congregations of Brothers filling this qualification, seven indicated their willingness to cooperate and their interest in the findings of the study. These eight congregations of Brothers had 11 independent provincial or general motherhouses involved. The same procedure was used as with the Sisters. The major superiors of the Brothers were requested to send the names of prospective respondents and these lists served as the source for the Brothers actively participating.

The total group of respondents represented a wide range of teaching experience. The mean number of years experience for each group was as follows: (a) Sisters, 25.9 years; (b) priests, 7.5 years; and (c) Brothers, 19.3 years. Academic backgrounds were also widely divergent, as Table 2 shows.

According to *The 1960 Catholic Directory,* the full-time teaching corps in the Catholic school system consisted of 98,471 Sisters, 10,890 priests, and 4,778 Brothers. Lay teachers were not included here since the objective of the study was the productivity of religious vocations. The total number of respondents in terms of percentage of total teaching body was as follows: .6 per cent of the Sisters, .3 per cent of the priests, and .84 per cent of the Brothers. When percentages for priests

TABLE 2

ACADEMIC BACKGROUND OF RESPONDENTS

Type	Sisters	Mean Percentages of Priests	Brothers
BA or equivalent	20.9	30.3	5.0
MA or equivalent	67.3	60.6	70.0
MA pending	9.0	6.1	17.5
Ph. D.	1.9	3.0	0.0
Ph. D. pending	.9	0.0	7.5

and Brothers were merged, the result was .57 per cent of the male religious teachers in the system. Prorated on the basis of 10,000 such teachers, the data read: for the population responding, 60 out of every 10,000 Sister teachers and 57 out of every 10,000 male religious teachers participated in the study. These percentages were close enough to warrant the assertion that the study represents fairly equalized sectors of the general religious teaching body in the United States.

MATERIALS

The problem was investigated in terms of: (a) a data sheet directed to the major superiors of those congregations in the United States engaged in secondary education; and (b) a self-constructed questionnaire devised for three groups of respondents: Sisters, priests, and Brothers. The next section of this chapter will describe these two instruments of inquiry.

Data Sheet

The schedule was constructed with a view to obtaining from the 142 communities information about their members in various categories (postulants, novices, junior professed and finally professed Sisters). Its principal objective was to secure data concerning the high-school environment of their postulants, novices, and junior professed Sisters. The school types listed on the data sheet were: the aspirancy, public high school, parish high school, central high school for girls, central coeducational high school, and central co-institutional high school. Because some might have entered religious life from an educational level other than high school, a separate section was included which provided for those who had entered from junior or senior colleges and graduate or professional fields. These areas were then grouped under the corresponding high school types listed above. The major superiors were also asked to indicate on the data sheet the number of high schools of each type they were currently staffing to determine possible relationships between the number of schools staffed and the number of religious vocations received from these schools.

Questionnaire

Before answering the questionnaire proper, respondents were asked to complete a preliminary section of general information concerning their academic background and their professional preparation and experience. Provision was made for data showing their status, whether principal, co- or assistant-principal, teacher, or counselor. They were also invited to reveal their total teaching and administrative experience in terms of years, and to atomize their total secondary school experience according to length of service in the various types of high schools used throughout the study.

The most important part of the questionnaire and the core of the entire research was a small section labeled "for administrative personnel only." Qualified respondents were to indicate here the total enrollment, total faculty, and total vocation output for the years 1954-1959. An opportunity was also given to enumerate the possible vocation output for 1959-1960, but these figures were not included in the statistical analysis because they were more likely to represent wishful thinking than a *fait accompli*.

Part I of the Questionnaire. The questionnaire was arranged in three main sections. Part I, directed mainly to the personal history of the respondents' vocations, sought to ascertain the source of their first thoughts on the religious life, the time when this occurred, the period of their final decision, and the date of their entrance to the seminary or the religious life. Also requested was the type of high school they attended. If coeducational, they were asked to indicate what influence, if any, this type of school had on their vocation choice. Then in order to gauge the extent of the influence of school environment on their views and impressions, respondents were asked what general school atmosphere made the strongest impression on them. Because teacher personality was an hypothetical construct in the development of religious vocations and was awaiting confirmation as an influential factor in this respect, the implications of teacher personality and related aspects were sought in the question: "If you did not join the Order to which your teachers belonged, what reasons could you give?"

Another attempt to measure personality influence came through No. 2 of Part I, which sought to assess the relative influence of 19 selected factors in the respondents' choice of a vocation to the religious life. Respondents were asked to designate these factors as of "very great influence," "considerable influence," "slight influence," or "no influence." In No. 3 of Part I, respondents were requested to name the obstacles blocking the realization of their vocations. Sixteen such factors were suggested. These were to be evaluated as "greatest obstacle," "considerable obstacle," "slight obstacle," or "no obstacle." In the same section, the respondents were asked to repeat the evaluation, but in the light of youth's difficulties today. Material in Part I of the questionnaire owed much to the study made by Bowdern (1936). It thus served as a basis for comparing the situation in the thirties with that which prevails in the present era. Although partly personal in nature, Part I referred primarily to vocational implications in the school situation as experienced by the respondents. The confidential nature of the replies was respected, and the data lost their personal significance through their anonymity and the statistical techniques to which they were subjected.

Part II of the Questionaire. Part II contained statements regarding certain aspects of secondary education, with emphasis on single-sex versus coeducational systems.   The statements contained implications for the development of vocations in Catholic high schools.   Respondents were to check their opinions with appropriate symbols as follows:

A—Complete agreement with the statement

B—Strong inclination to agree but with reservations

C—Inclination to disagree rather than to agree

D—Strong disagreement

X—Not in a position to judge

Part II was divided into three areas: *General Statements, Statements Regarding the Vocation Aspects of Secondary Education, and Statements Regarding the Teaching Aspects of Secondary Education.*   From these expressions of opinion it was hoped to educe patterns of thought specific to the four main categories of respondents, according to which the data were classified: Sisters in coeducational schools (SCD), Sisters in single-sex schools (SSS), priests principally engaged in the coeducational system (PCD), and Brothers almost exclusively working in the single-sex type (BSS).

Part III of the Questionnaire.   Since learning involves many intangibles which have repercussions in teacher-student rapport, and since such rapport is a weighty factor in developing the confidence and sympathy which are so effective in promoting religious vocations, the investigator designed Part III to measure certain factors in this area.   These factors were divided into two parts: *Regarding the Teacher* and *Regarding the Student.*   Those aspects were chosen which affect both teacher and pupil as they impinge on each other's personalities during the educative process, thus indirectly influencing vocation choice.   Under *Regarding the Teacher,* two phases were included: (a) factors that contribute to successful teaching of adolescents in high school, and (b) factors that were a source of difficulty for the respondents on the secondary level. Eighteen items were suggested as possibly conducing to effective teaching of high-school adolescents.   These were to be rated as "highly important; strongly recommended," "desirable, helpful," "of slight value," or "of no value." Of the 18 possibilities offered, 11 related directly in some way or other to the personality of the teacher, while the remaining seven were concerned with aspects of administration.

Twenty-two items were offered for evaluation as factors that might have placed the respondents under strain in the classroom, thus militating against the ideal "teacher image" of dedicated professional competence which should inspire youth to imitation. The factors were to be rated as they were a source of difficulty in the respondents' experience in secondary schools. Values were to be assigned as follows:

A—Very great difficulty

B—Considerable difficulty

C—Slight difficulty

D—No difficulty

X—No experience with this factor

Since several factors had implications for the coeducational versus single-sex problem of the major hypothesis, it was hoped through this section to produce further data to strengthen the arguments in favor of single-sex schools.

Regarding the Student, in four differentiated sections, probed the thinking of the respondents concerning: (a) guidance areas, (b) school subjects, (c) school-type preferences, and (d) needs of secondary school students. Nine suggested guidance areas were offered for evaluation as to their effectiveness for mixed group guidance. The scale of values included: "best," "next best," "least," and "not for mixed groups."

Eleven school subjects also came within the range of respondent evaluation. Religion, chemistry, English, mathematics, physics, Latin, biology, music, art, commercial subjects, and foreign languages were to be judged by the respondents as to their effectiveness with combined groups of boys and girls. Space was provided to include any subjects other than those listed if the respondents so desired.

Another area investigated was the preferences of teachers and administrators for school types according to the three following categories: (a) personal preference, (b) preferred for optimum development of the adolescent personality, and (c) preferred for fostering religious vocations. The school types from which choice was to be made were: (a) parish high school, (b) private high school, (c) central high school for either boys or girls, (d) central coeducational high school, and (e) central co-institutional high school. The sex status of the central high school for either boys or girls, central coeducational high school, and central co-institutional high school was evident from their type name. Parish high schools were considered coeducational, and private high schools were assumed to be single-sex, since in both these cases the arrangement mentioned is the usual one.

Because the study sought to point out the possible causes for the great discrepancy in vocations from the single-sex schools and those that are coeducational, the investigator looked for clues in the attitudes of respondents to suggested needs of the secondary school student. Sixteen areas were tentatively offered for evaluation, with provision made for write-ins according to the judgment of the respondents.

The last section of the questionnaire consisted of five open-end questions which provided for a wide range of expression concerning most of the problems that had been covered in objective fashion in various sections of the research instrument. The questions referred to: (a) teaching methods of the Sisters in mixed groups, (b) the need of the adolescent girl for separate schools, (c) age at which boys should be taught exclusively by men, (d) helps and/or hindrances to the development of religious vocations in the type of school in which the respondents were currently situated, (e) advantages and disadvantages for boys and girls in mixed classes, (f) traits of the ideal teacher, (g) the relationship between present vocation needs and current practices in Catholic secondary education, and (h) suggestions for effecting a change of policy if such be needed.

PROCEDURES

The final achievement of the study's main objective neces-
sitated the use of suitable procedural techniques.   A descrip-
tion of those used in the investigation follows.

Contacting Religious Communities

As an introductory step, the cooperation of the major superiors of 200 congregations engaged in secondary education
was enlisted.   These persons were approached by mail with an
explanation of the nature of the project.   The 142 cooperating
religious superiors represented as many independent units of
teaching Sisters, distributed geographically throughout 45
states and the District of Columbia.   Table 3 illustrates the

TABLE 3

SCHOOL DISTRIBUTION BY REGIONS

Region	No. of Schools
New England: Maine, New Hampshire, Vermont, Massachusetts, Rhode Island, Connecticut	32
Middle Atlantic: New York, New Jersey, Delaware, Pennsylvania, Maryland, Virginia, West Virginia	72
Southern: North Carolina, South Carolina, Georgia, Florida, Alabama, Mississippi, Louisiana, Texas, Oklahoma, Arkansas, Tennessee	27
East Central: Ohio, Indiana, Illinois, Kentucky, Michigan, Wisconsin	74
West Central: Minnesota, Iowa, Missouri, Kansas, Nebraska, North Dakota, South Dakota	79
Northwestern: Montana, Wyoming, Idaho, Washington, Oregon	12
Southwestern: Colorado, New Mexico, Utah, Arizona, Nevada, California	29
District of Columbia	3

regional spread of the participating schools.   The superiors responded favorably, expressing their interest in the study and

their willingness to be of assistance in providing data. As indication of their interest, 135 expressed a desire to have the results of the research reported to them. These religious superiors were encouraged to participate, not only by their own interest and the urgency of the problem, but also by the assurance that all data would be treated confidentially and anonymously.

Contacting Prospective Respondents

The lists evolving from the religious congregations contacted in the preliminary stage of the survey produced the names of 701 Sisters who were available for research purposes. During the last week in April, 1960, an explanatory letter, together with a copy of the questionnaire, was sent to each of these persons, with a request for cooperation. Seventy-seven Sisters who lived within easy reach of the investigator were also approached through private and group interviews. The total participating group of Sisters reached 595, after a follow-up had corralled a number of diffident respondents.

Several of the religious superiors had sent, either advertently or otherwise, the names of priest-principals or priest-counselors in charge of several high schools staffed by their communities. These 28 priests received the same explanatory letter and a copy of the questionnaire, with the request to participate and thus lend the research the benefit of their knowledge and experience. The remaining five priests were approached personally. The 40 Brothers were contacted in exactly the same way as the Sisters: (a) through the medium of *The 1960 Catholic Directory,* (b) letters requesting permission directed to the major superiors of the respective congregations of Brothers, (c) the acquisition of lists of names of Brothers who would be prospective respondents to the questionnaire, (d) mailing of the explanatory letter and the research schedule. One Brother, in addition to the 40 referred to previously, sent such an incomplete response that his contribution had to be discarded.

Sorting the Responses

After the Sisters' questionnaires had been returned, they were sorted into two basic categories: single-sex and coeducational. These two groups were further subdivided into parish, central, and private. The largest representation was found in the parish coeducational high schools and the private single-sex high schools. Least representative were the private coeducational high schools and the central high schools for girls.

Compilation of Core Data

When the classification into specific categories had been completed, enrollments and religious vocations for the years 1954-1959 were calculated to serve as a basis for comparison between the two fundamental groups: single-sex and coeducational. Figures resulting from these calculations were submitted to tests of significance.

The religious communities had been requested to provide information about the previous high-school experience of their postulants, novices, and junior professed Sisters. The data from the archives of the participating religious communities were translated into percentages for the school types represented on the data sheet. Apart from this simple treatment, no other statistical device was applied to the data here concerned, since they served only as a basis for comparison with and emphasis of the data evolving from the five-year records of the participating high schools.

Statistical Techniques with Opinion Data

Part I of the questionnaire with its personal implications for the religious vocations of the respondents, relied on the use of mean percentages to elicit meaning from the data submitted. Factors influencing the choice of a vocation to the priesthood or to the religious life were evaluated according to the following scale:

5—Very great influence

3—Considerable influence

1—Slight influence

0—No influence

All positive values (5, 3, and 1) were combined and the mean percentages of choices calculated. Obstacles to the realization of a religious vocation were assessed according to a similar scale:

5—Greatest obstacle

3—Considerable obstacle

1—Slight obstacle

0—No obstacle

Results were expressed in terms of mean percentages of respondents rating certain factors as "greatest obstacle." These percentages were then used as the basis for comparison between obstacles confronting the subjects of the study and those hindrances which retard religious vocations today.

As a tangent to the major thesis which concerned school environment as a factor in stimulating or deterring religious vocations, the 51 statements in Part II of the questionnaire were used to explore the possibility of environmental pressures on the opinions and value choices of the respondents. For this purpose, the groupings of SCD, SSS, PCD, and BSS were matched in various combinations to emphasize the degree of relationship between groupings according to same sex and same environment. Chi squares were computed. Seven of the 153 groupings were significant at the .01 level, 15 at the .05 level, and eight approached significance with chi squares over three for one degree of freedom. The 15 most discriminating and the 15 least discriminating items were grouped for the purpose of discovering patterns of opinions which might depend causally on teaching environment. Since no effort had been made to control several variables, such as age, experience, etc., the results cannot be considered conclusive, even for the sample in question. A trend, however, may be discerned and serve as an incentive for future research in this area.

It might be objected that the statements were evaluated in terms of preferred judgments. It is the opinion of the investigator that these judgments of preference are functions of environment. If the resulting chi squares proved significant differences according to patterns of teaching environment, then by analogy the conclusion might be applied to vocation choices of adolescents in varying school environments.

The procedure followed in analyzing the data from Part II was as follows. All statements were judged on the basis of a scale of five values:

A—Complete agreement with the statement
B—Strong inclination to agree but with reservations
C—Inclination to disagree rather than to agree
D—Strong disagreement
X—Not in a position to judge

Frequency of response to each item was recorded and converted into percentages. Values A and B were combined and designated as the equivalent of a "true" or "yes" reaction to the statement in question. These combined A and B percentages served as a basis for the intergroup comparisons concerning the value choices of Part II.

Part III of the questionnaire concerned factors in the learning situation as concomitant variables in the production of vocation choices. *Regarding the Teacher* contained 18 such variables which might contribute to or militate against the successful teaching of adolescents in high school. Some items were oriented to a psychological frame of reference, while others were geared toward administrative aspects of the teaching situation. The following four items discriminated most effectively among the four specially classified groups of respondents and were singled out for special treatment:

(a) teacher of the same sex as students
(b) separate schools for each sex
(c) separate classes for each sex
(d) mingling of the sexes in class

With the special relevance which each of these items contained for the main hypothesis of the research, each rated special statistical consideration. The scale for evaluating these factors in the successful teaching of adolescents ranged from five to zero.

5—Highly important; strongly recommended
3—Desirable, helpful
1—Slight value
0—No value

Percentages of choices of "5" and "3" were combined and classified as "yes" responses. They were then used as a basis for comparison among the four respondent groups: SCD, SSS, PCD, and BSS. Chi squares were computed for each of the matched groups and significant differences noted for the relationships between them.

Twenty-two factors were suggested as possibly militating against the production of an ideal "teacher image," either because of pressures engendered in the classroom itself, or because of burdens placed upon teachers with consequent repercussions in the learning situation. Values in this section ranged as follows:

5—Very great difficulty
3—Considerable difficulty
1—Slight difficulty
0—No difficulty
X—No experience with this factor

Value choices of "5" and "3" were merged for each of the four groups: SCD, SSS, PCD, and BSS. Rank-difference correlation techniques were applied. A composite percentage was also computed for the combined groups of respondents and the factors arranged in rank order according to these percentages.

Tangential to the main topic of religious vocations and school environment, the two succeeding areas of Part III of the questionnaire related to guidance and school subjects as they bear on the problem of religious vocations in Catholic secondary schools. Guidance areas were evaluated in terms of suitability for mixed groups of boys and girls. The value scale ranged from "best for mixed groups" through two intermediate values to "not for mixed groups." Again, percentages of choices were computed and from the resultant picture judgments were formed concerning the effectiveness of certain guidance areas for coeducational schools. For both the guidance areas and the school subjects, *rho* correlations were computed.

In the section which elicited the school-type preferences of the participants, the procedure adopted involved a threefold arrangement: (a) computations of the percentages of choices for each type of school (parish, private, central for either sex, central coeducational, and central co-institutional), from each group of respondents (SCD, SSS, PCD, and BSS), in three categories of choice (personal preference, optimum development of adolescent personality, and best environment for fostering religious vocations); (b) transmutation of these percentages into ranks for each school type, each group of respondents, and each category of choice; (c) calculations of *rho* correlations for several combinations of respondents and in each of the three categories.

Comparisons basic to the *rho* correlations were:

SCD and SSS)
) Comparisons based on similarity
PCD and BSS)   of sex

SCD and PCD)
) Comparisons based on similarity
SSS and BSS)   of teaching environment

Tests of significance were applied to the raw data for the preferential category, "Best environment for religious vocations," since this area was the special interest of the study. Line graphs were also used to illustrate relationships between respondent groups.

In the area of student needs, mean percentages were calculated from the opinions of respondents. Only those percentages were used as a basis for comparison which were gathered from the first two values on the scale: 5—very great need; 3—considerable need. These percentages were then resolved into ranks and *rho* correlations computed. Because of its particular significance to the study, Item No. 9 (Chance to mingle with the opposite sex in class) was submitted to the chi-square test of significance. As a variation of the usual four-group respondent division, the opinions of the subjects were considered according to another set of categories, including the usual quadruple arrangement:

(a) Sisters in coeducational schools
(b) Sisters in single-sex schools
(c) Priests in coeducational schools
(d) Brothers in single-sex schools
(e) All the Sisters in both types
(f) Priests and Brothers combined
(g) All coeducational teachers (Sisters and priests)
(h) All single-sex teachers (Sisters and Brothers)

Comparisons were based on the following groupings: a and b; c and d; e and f; g and h. Tests of significance were applied to these data.

Information from the open-end questions was transformed into percentages and fitted into the general structure wherever it had special relevance. Whatever had only slight connection with the main interest of the study was incorporated in a general way in the summary.

CHAPTER IV

ANALYSIS AND DISCUSSION

The primary aim of the present investigation was to explore the relationship between single-sex and coeducational high schools with respect to their productivity of religious vocations. To provide an answer to the question under investigation, three groups of Catholic educators were selected as sources of data. The groups chosen represented diversified faculties with teaching and/or administrative experience in Catholic secondary schools: (a) Sisters in single-sex and coeducational high schools, (b) priests predominantly engaged in the coeducational field, and (c) Brothers exclusively operating in single-sex institutions. Since the main interest of the thesis concerned schools and religious vocations as they related to the teaching Sister, the priests and Brothers who participated served simply as bases for comparison in the opinion section of the questionnaire. Because attitudes and opinions may arise both from the sex of the subjects and from their teaching environments, the Sisters participating in the survey were further subdivided into: (a) Sisters teaching in coeducational schools (SCD), and (b) Sisters teaching in single-sex schools (SSS).

The present research was designed to test the following major hypothesis and three subsidiary hypotheses:

1. Since coeducation in high school influences girls during their most impressionable years, a relationship could be expected to exist between type of high school and productivity of religious vocations.

2. Psychological differences between the sexes would indicate that the most fruitful environment for religious vocations of students in secondary schools is offered when teachers are of the same sex as their students.

3. Teacher respondents would prefer the teacher to be of the same sex as the pupil for vocation purposes.

61

4.   One of the strongest influences in fostering vocations to the religious life is the personality of the religious teacher.

The first hypothesis depended for confirmation on factual data from 328 participating schools and 142 religious congregations.   Flowing from the first as a corollary and dependent upon it for confirmation, the second hypothesis relied on the same factual data from the participating schools.   The third hypothesis likewise stemmed from the first and was confirmed through the opinions of the 668 respondents who voiced their preferences for the single-sex school system as the best for the development of religious vocations.   The fourth hypothesis, which referred to teacher personality as an important ingredient in the complex of influences fostering vocations, was strengthened through the almost unanimous consensus of respondent opinions and also through the personal-history data of the Sisters taking part in the survey.

A.   *First Hypothesis — Analysis*

The burden of the thesis was the comparative contribution to religious vocations of the two fundamental types of school systems, single-sex and coeducational.   The results can be grouped into: (a) two sets of factual data on religious vocations as revealed by school records for 1954-1959, and archives of religious congregations for the years 1949-1959; and (b) the opinions of Sisters, priests, and Brothers concerning the religious-vocation aspects of Catholic secondary education.

1.   *Factual Data from High Schools.*   The total number of vocations to the sisterhoods originating between 1954-1959 in the 328 participating schools was studied as to point of origin, whether single-sex or coeducational schools.   These data, which were sought in the first part of the questionnaire, are presented in Tables 4, 5, and 6, and reveal a striking confirmation of the major hypothesis, namely, that a relationship could be expected to exist between the type of high school and the productivity of religious vocations.   School records from 1954-1959 revealed that the number of religious **vocations** from the 151 participating all-girls schools numbered 3,817

TABLE 4

COMPARISONS BASED ON ENROLLMENT AND NO. OF VOCATIONS IN SINGLE-SEX HIGH SCHOOLS

	No. of Students and Schools	Size	No. of Vocations	% of Vocations	Difference	Chi Square
Parish	1. 6629 (10)	Below 200	83	1.26	1 & 2	5.668 *
	2. 18426 (12)	200 plus	167	.91	1 & 3	.315
	3. 5371 (2)	500 plus	74	1.38	2 & 3	9.439 **
	30426 (24)		324	Mn= 1.18		
Central	4. 13248 (7)	200 plus	135	1.02	4 & 5	1.103
	5. 11507 (3)	500 plus	102	.89	4 & 6	1.128
	6. 71256 (6)	1000 plus	800	1.12	5 & 6	5.046 *
	96011 (16)		1037	Mn= 1.01		
Private	7. 16411 (31)	Below 200	316	1.93	7 & 8	37.821 **
	8. 74143 (48)	200 plus	957	1.29	7 & 9	75.561 **
	9. 99375 (30)	500 plus	1104	1.11	7 & 10	75.617 **
	10. 11752 (2)	1000 plus	79	.57	8 & 9	11.465 **
					8 & 10	32.084 **
					9 & 10	28.802 **
	201681 (111)		2456	Mr= 1.25		
Totals:	328118 (151)		3817	Mn= 1.16		

** Significant at .01 level
* Significant at .05 level

TABLE 5

COMPARISONS BASED ON ENROLLMENT AND NO. OF VOCATIONS IN
COEDUCATIONAL HIGH SCHOOLS

	No. of Students and Schools	Size	% of Girls	No. of Voc.	% of Voc.	Difference	Chi Square
Parish	1. 17448 (82)	Below 200	51.5	179	1.03	1 & 2	8.875 **
	2. 19475 (26)	200 plus	54.5	143	.73	1 & 3	6.504 *
	3. 7528 (5)	500 plus	54.4	52	.69	2 & 3	.190
	44451			374 Mn=	.82		
Central	4. 3388 (9)	Below 200	55.5	44	1.29	4 & 5	8.312 **
	5. 13070 (17)	200 plus	51.4	101	.77	4 & 6	33.307 **
	6. 18909 (14)	500 plus	52.6	90	.48	4 & 7	32.462 **
	7. 23405 (7)	1000 plus	53.5	117	.50	5 & 6	11.171 **
						5 & 7	10.325 **
						6 & 7	.153
	58772 (47)			352 Mn=	.76		
Private	8. 2343 (7)	Below 200	56.4	25	1.07	8 & 9	1.086
	9. 3571 (5)	200 plus	57.6	29	.81	8 & 10	2.332
	10. 7103 (4)	500 plus	55.7	54	.76	8 & 11	1.836
	11. 3286 (1)	1000 plus	55.1	24	.73		
	16303 (17)			132 Mn=	.84		
Totals:	119526 (177)			858 Mn=	.81		

** Significant at .01 level
* Significant at .05 level

for the five-year period; 177 coeducational schools produced 858 vocations to the sisterhoods during the same length of time. Total enrollment in the all-girls schools numbered 328,118; in the coeducational group, the enrollment was 119,526. The mean percentage of religious vocations for the all-girls schools was 1.16; for the coeducational schools, .81. The differences between the percentage totals for the all-girls and the coeducational schools were highly significant at the .01 level.

Before elaborating on the various significant chi squares to be discussed as the chapter progresses, it may be well to note that significant differences merely indicate the *fact* of the difference, not the *cause,* except by inference or implication. As Lindquist (1940) notes, a statistically significant difference is not necessarily a reliable difference. It indicates merely that chance fluctuation is not operative. Unwarranted generalizations in the interpretation of causes are to be avoided, therefore, even though the data may point to obvious trends.

To increase the reliability of the differences, the two systems were paired in various combinations. Comparisons were based on the following schema:

1. Total coeducational enrollment and total all-girls enrollment

2. Subdivisions into parish, central, and private:
   parish coeducational—parish all-girls
   central coeducational—central all-girls
   private coeducational—private all-girls

3. Enrollment—coeducational versus all-girls
   coeducational, below 200—all-girls, below 200
   coeducational, 200 plus—all-girls, 200 plus
   coeducational, 500 plus—all-girls, 500 plus
   coeducational, 1000 plus—all-girls, 1000 plus

4. Enrollment *within* each of the two systems

The chi square for the relationship between total number of vocations from coeducational high schools and the total number from all-girls high schools was 165.7196, highly significant for one degree of freedom. Table 6 shows results when parish coed and parish all-girls, central coed and central all-girls, and private coed and private all-girls schools were matched, comparisons based chiefly on sex placement. Further adaptations of the matching process paired the most representative of both types as well as the least representative of both. All chi squares were highly significant. In each case, differences favored the all-girls schools.

TABLE 6

COMPARISONS BETWEEN ALL-GIRLS AND COEDUCATIONAL
SCHOOLS IN VOCATION PRODUCTION

Comparison	Chi Square
Total coed schools — total all-girls schools:	
Parish coed—parish all-girls	9.587
Central coed—central all-girls	93.469
Private coed—private all-girls	21.072
Most representative:	
Parish coed (113)—private all-girls (111)	44.407
Least representative:	
Private coed (17)—central all-girls (16)	9.568

Chi square $= \dfrac{3.841 \text{ at } .05 \text{ level of confidence}}{6.635 \text{ at } .01 \text{ level of confidence}}$ Df $= 1$.

To insure even greater reliability, the two types were matched according to size. Four classifications were arbitrarily chosen to fit the data: (a) enrollments below 200, (b) 200 plus, (c) 500 plus, and (d) 1000 plus. In each enrollment category, all-girls schools and coeducational schools were matched against each other. All differences were highly significant in favor of the all-girls schools. The all-girls schools with an enrollment below 200 and coeducational schools below 200 yielded a significant chi square of 35.263. The 200-plus category produced a chi square of 46.356; the 500-plus group, 69.310; and the 1000-plus class, 60.581 (Table 7). In each instance, the differences arose from a higher vocation yield of the all-girls schools. In no case did a coeducational school approach the percentage yield of religious vocations in the all-girls schools. The lowest mean percentage in the all-girls schools was 1.01, coming from the central girls' high schools. The highest mean percentage for the coeducational schools was .842, coming from the private schools. The highest mean percentage of the coeducational system did not reach the lowest mean percentage of the all-girls schools.

TABLE 7

RELATIONSHIPS BETWEEN COEDUCATIONAL AND ALL-GIRLS HIGH SCHOOLS WITH COMPARABLE ENROLL-MENTS IN RESPECT TO VOCATION PRODUCTIVITY

Size	Chi Square
Below 200	35.263
200 plus	46.356
500 plus	69.310
1000 plus	60.581

Chi square $= \begin{array}{l} 3.841 \text{ at } .05 \text{ level of confidence} \\ 6.635 \text{ at } .01 \text{ level of confidence} \end{array}$ Df $= 1$.

Another variation of the relationships was based on enrollment comparisons *within* the single-sex and the coeducational types of administration. Table 8 indicates the relative stand of the several groupings. In both classifications, single-sex and coeducational, the smallest schools showed the greatest percentage of success in promoting religious vocations. This points to a possible relationship between size of school and number of vocations. It might be safe to assume that stronger teacher-pupil relationships in the smaller schools could be a factor in the vocation promotion programs of the smaller schools. Other reasons for assuming that size of school influences a girl's attitude toward religious life in general may lie in the rich extra-curricular programs and the manifold social opportunities of the larger schools. Where the institution is

TABLE 8

RELATIONSHIPS BASED ON ENROLLMENT FIGURES
WITHIN GROUPS

Enrollment	% of Vocations	Difference	Chi Square
Coeducational			
1. Below 200	1.12		
2. 200 plus	.77	1 & 2	15.735
3. 500 plus	.64	1 & 3	40.878
4. 1000 plus	.61	1 & 4	46.206
All-Girls			
1. Below 200	1.59		
2. 200 plus	1.07	1 & 2	42.272
3. 500 plus	1.13	1 & 3	62.646
5. 1000 plus	.89	1 & 4	66.598

Chi square = 3.841 at .05 level of confidence
6.635 at .01 level of confidence   Df = 1.

small, the meager budget and the narrowed intramural social contacts prohibit large-scale extra-curricular activities.

The conclusions for the coeducational schools are most valid for the parish type, since 113 of these parish schools participated in the survey, as contrasted with 47 central coeducational and 17 private coeducational schools. The conclusions for the single-sex schools, on the contrary, are most valid for the private-school type, with 111 of the latter represented in the study, contrasted with 24 parish single-sex and 16 central single-sex schools. The data would seem to indicate then that the size of the school has greatest impact on vocation production in private single-sex schools and central coeducational schools. (See Tables 4 and 5.) In both these settings, single-sex or coeducational, the results are the same: vocation percentages decrease as enrollments increase.

A ten-year study (Sister Mary Teresa Francis, 1960) conducted in the Midwest showed similar findings with respect to the relationship between enrollment and religious vocations. These effects are apparent in the enrollment-vocation percentages as presented by Sister Mary Teresa Francis. The following tabulation includes, in parentheses, the vocation percentages of the present study.

	All-Girls	*Coed*
Small (below 200)	5.11 (1.59)	2.18 (1.12)
Medium-sized (200 plus)	5.18 (1.07)	1.47 (0.77)
Large (500 plus and 1000 plus)	3.64 (1.03)	.62 (0.63)

In order to compare the findings of the present investigation with the results of the Midwest study in the specific area of enrollment and vocations, the investigator merged the "500-plus" and the "1000-plus" categories of the present study, the better to compare them with the "large" groupings of the cited research. The "200-plus" classification was considered on a par with the "medium" group, while the "below 200" and the "small" categories were judged comparable. These adjusted groupings of the present research followed the enrollment divisions of the cited study. Despite the almost negligible percentage increase for medium-sized all-girl schools in the Midwest study, the same general pattern prevails in both: vocations are in inverse ratio to school enrollment, no matter whether the administration be single-sex or coeducational. The basic vocation percentage, however, remains higher in the all-girls schools.

The present research would seem to give factual support to the observations of Bowdern (1936): (a) vocation-subjects in his research did not attend coeducational high schools; (b) vocation-boys were taught by men and vocation-girls were taught by women. Bowdern had recommended that coeducation should be discouraged in the Catholic school system and stressed the need for separate classes at least.

Although the present research was concentrated on girls, some support can be drawn from it for Coleman's research (1960). Coleman analyzed the effects of school environment on interest in and development of vocations among boys in the two fundamental types of his study: all-boys and boy-girl schools. His statistics did not indicate any appreciable difference between the two types of schools as sources of vocations to seminaries and novitiates. The sampling was small (30 schools), and the difference between the two types, as indicated by their percentages of vocations to enrollments, might have been augmented in favor of single-sex schools had the sample been larger. Coleman's percentages for the all-boys and the coeducational schools were 4.2 and 3.7, respectively. Here again the trend is apparent, namely, more vocations come from single-sex than from coeducational schools.

Findings of the present study, in which it was noted that the larger the coeducational school the fewer the vocations and the lower the vocation percentage, did not support the results of Shocklee's investigation (1957). Shocklee found the 83 coeducational high schools in his study producing religious vocations at the rate of three per cent of the enrollment. The larger schools had slightly greater percentages. However, the comparatively large percentage of vocations in Shocklee's sample represents coverage of both male and female student population. Shocklee's data were contaminated for use in the present comparisons because he included both sexes in his evaluation. However, since Coleman also found no appreciable difference between the two basic types of schools in the production of boys' vocations, it might be plausible to hold that where boys enter the picture for comparative purposes, the percentage will rise, since the coeducational atmosphere does not seem to affect them as it does the more impressionable maturity of a school's female population.

2. *Factual Data from Religious Communities.* A related aspect of the research involved the school origins of the religious subjects, postulants, novices, and junior professed Sisters, in 142 participating religious communities. Major superiors of these communities were asked to supply data from their archives concerning the type of high school previously attended by their religious members. Table 9 shows the general nature of this part of the study. Vocations thus listed as en-

TABLE 9

HIGH-SCHOOL SOURCES OF RELIGIOUS VOCATIONS
IN 142 CONGREGATIONS

Type	*No. of Vocations & Community Schools		% of Voc.	**No.of Voc.	% of Voc.
Aspirancy	1797	(49)	14.31	1797	12.56
Public H. S.	1439		11.46	2139	14.95
Parish H. S.	2499	(460)	19.90	2877	20.11
Private H. S.	4239	(218)	33.51	4728	33.05
Central Girls' H. S.	1483	(56)	11.81	1564	10.93
Central Coed. H. S.	952	(140)	7.58	1038	7.26
Central Co-inst. H. S.	151	(31)	1.20	163	1.14
	12560		99.77	14306	100.00

* Excludes entrants from college, graduate, or professional levels
** Includes entrants from college, graduate, or professional levels

tering directly from high school numbered 12,560 for a time
period of approximately ten years, 1949-1959. Corroborating
the statistics supplied by the high-school records, the data from
the religious communities also showed that 4,239 or 33.5 per
cent of these vocations to the teaching sisterhoods in the sample studied came from private high schools. To these might be
added 1,483 or 11.8 per cent from girls' central high schools.
These two single-sex types were the educational environment
for 45.3 per cent of the vocations under scrutiny. If to this
percentage were added those vocations which arrived by way
of the aspirancy, which is also a single-sex situation, the total
would be 59.6 per cent evolving from single-sex schools. The
chi square computed from the raw data emerging as vocations
from central girls' high schools and central coeducational high
schools was 107.763, highly significant at the .01 level of confidence. As evident from the data in Table 9, the percentages
of religious vocations from the various school sources arranged

themselves into the approximations of a normal distribution curve.

Inclusion of the data from post-high school sources notably raised the vocation percentage of public high schools. Such increase, however, may point to the influence of junior and senior colleges in promoting vocation consciousness among those not previously exposed to it in public schools. Junior and senior colleges produced 1,180 vocations in the sample surveyed. As one respondent among the major superiors remarked, the junior college conducted by her community is its most prolific source of vocations.

To summarize the analysis of the major hypothesis, the factual data of this research substantiated the principal thesis which stated that a relationship could be found between type of high school and the number of religious vocations. All findings pointed conclusively to the superiority of the single-sex school in this respect. Among the several types of single-sex administration (parish, central, private), the private high school was clearly in the lead in providing new candidates for the religious life in the various sisterhoods. The two chief sources for these conclusions were: (a) the actual vocation count provided by the high-school records of 151 single-sex high schools and 177 coeducational high schools, and (b) the number of members in the 142 participating religious communities who had previously attended various types of single-sex high schools, with the private single-sex type providing the majority of vocations.

B. *Second Hypothesis — Analysis*

One of the three subsidiary hypotheses of the present investigation held that because of the psychological differences between the sexes, the most fruitful environment for the religious vocations of students in secondary schools is offered when teachers are of the same sex as their students. Because of the higher percentage of vocations of students in all-girls schools and the significant differences between them and the coeducational schools in this respect, the conclusion might be safely drawn that all-girls schools are more fruitful in the productivity of religious vocations than their coeducational counterparts. Since the all-girls schools were staffed almost exclusively by Sisters and laywomen, a cautious corollary might flow from these findings, namely, that when teachers are of the same sex as their students, it is easier to influence the latter's thinking in the direction of religious idealism. The hypothesis in question received strong support from the factual data directly bearing on the vocation productivity of the 328 schools studied.

C. *Third Hypothesis — Analysis*

According to the third hypothesis, for vocation purposes teacher respondents would prefer the teacher to be of the same sex as the students. To probe their thinking on this matter, respondents were asked, in Part III of the research instrument, to indicate their school preferences in three categories.

Opinion Data. Bolstering the factual data revealed by the school records and the archives of the religious congregations were the opinions and evaluations offered by respondents in sundry areas of the questionnaire. According to the views of the investigator, the value of the factual findings in the research would be considerably increased if the reflective opinions of professional educators would add further confirmation. The high productivity of vocations coming from single-sex schools as shown by the factual data was confirmed in the section devoted to teacher opinion. Throughout that section of the questionnaire which emphasized opinions and attitudes, the respondents were treated as four specific groups: (a) Sisters teaching in coeducational schools (SCD), (b) Sisters teaching in single-sex schools (SSS), (c) Priests teaching principally in coeducational schools (PCD), and (d) Brothers exclusively engaged in single-sex institutions (BSS). This division was made to evaluate better the choices of respondents with respect to their teaching environments. A subject might choose the type of environment to which she had become inured through close and constant association.

The school-type preferences requested in Part III required an evaluation of the environments provided by all five school types suggested in the list: parish, private, central single-sex, central coeducational, and central co-institutional. Parish high schools in the United States are usually coeducational, while private high schools are predominantly single-sex. Hence, it seemed sufficient to consider only these five main categories. Respondents were asked to express their preferences in three categories: (a) school type best suited for the development of religious vocations, (b) school type most conducive to the optimum development of the adolescent personality, and (c) school type personally preferred by the respondents. The combined groups of Sister teachers (595) selected schools as best suited for the favorable growth of religious vocations in the following order:

(a) private high school—selected by 41.95 per cent
(b) central single-sex high school—27.75 per cent
(c) parish high school—15.2 per cent
(d) central co-institutional high school—12.35 per cent
(e) central coeducational high school—2.2 per cent

Three types listed here, the private, the single-sex central, and the co-institutional, are sex-segregated, with special adaptations in the latter case. The total percentages of Sisters who chose any one of these three sex-segregated types for developing religious vocations reached 82.05, representing the opinions of eight out of every ten Sisters participating in the study.

Priests (33) in secondary education listed their preferences according to the following roster of percentages:

(a) central co-institutional high school—33.3 per cent
(b) central single-sex high school—30.3 per cent
(c) private high school—24.3 per cent
(d) parish, central coeducational high schools—each, 6.1 per cent

When the percentages of single-sex schools were combined, the result showed that 87.9 per cent of the priests favored a single-sex classroom atmosphere for fostering religious vocations. These data revealed that the parish high school is slowly becoming obsolete, as indicated by the low percentages of choice accorded this type. In confirmation of this trend, for the optimum development of the adolescent personality, the parish high school as a type rated only 9.7 per cent support among the Sisters (Table 10). It was next to last in the other two categories, "most conducive to the development of religious vocations," and "personal preference," being only slightly more popular in these respects than the coeducational central high school.

TABLE 10

SCHOOL-TYPE PREFERENCES

Type	SCD	SSS	PCD	BSS	Mean %-ages
Optimum Development of Religious Vocations					
1. Parish high school	13.8	17.8	6.1	9.3	11.75
2. Private high school	38.9	45.0	24.3	51.2	39.85
3. Central single-sex h. s.	27.2	28.3	30.3	32.5	29.60
4. Central coed. h.s.	4.4	0.0	6.1	0.0	2.62
5. Central co-inst. h. s.	15.8	8.9	33.3	7.0	16.25
Optimum Development of Adolescent Personality					
1. Parish high school	7.3	12.1	2.9	2.2	6.12
2. Private high school	15.6	27.4	14.7	55.6	28.32
3. Central single-sex h. s.	17.0	23.2	17.6	24.4	20.55
4. Central coed. h. s.	26.0	5.3	32.4	0.0	15.92
5. Central co-inst. h. s	34.1	32.1	32.4	17.8	29.10
Personal Preference					
1. Parish high school	23.5	16.5	6.9	2.2	12.27
2. Private high school	25.1	49.5	24.1	64.4	40.77
3. Central single-sex h. s.	18.3	22.5	6.9	26.7	18.60
4. Central coed. h. s.	16.5	2.0	17.2	0.0	8.92
5. Central co-inst. h. s.	16.5	9.5	44.8	6.7	19.37

The Brothers (40) signified the type of school they considered best for the nurture of religious vocations according to the following pattern:

(a) private high school—51.2 per cent
(b) central single-sex high school—32.5 per cent
(c) parish high school—9.3 per cent
(d) central co-institutional high school—7.0 per cent

The central coeducational high schools received a rating of zero from the Brothers in whatever category their preferences were sought. Combining the percentages of types of schools which teach the sexes separately, the Brothers preferred single-sex schools for the development of religious vocations in 90.7 per cent of their choices.

A large percentage (81.9) of Sisters in coeducational schools preferred the single-sex classroom atmosphere, whether private or central, for vocation purposes. An even greater percentage (82.2) of Sisters who taught in all-girls schools showed preference for this arrangement. The mean percentages of choices for each group of respondents are given in the following tabulation:

SCD	—	38.9 private	SSS	—	45.0 private
		27.2 central girls			28.3 central girls
		15.8 co-institutional			8.9 co-institutional
		——			——
		81.9			82.2
PCD	—	24.3 private	BSS	—	51.2 private
		30.3 central single-sex			32.5 central single-sex
		33.3 co-institutional			7.0 co-institutional
		——			——
		87.9			90.7

Surprisingly enough, since lobbying for single-sex education is commonly thought to issue from the ranks of the Sisters, priests and Brothers surpassed the Sisters in their expressed preferences for single-sex administration for vocation purposes. In order to high-light the favor enjoyed by the three single-sex types of administration as a suitable environment for fostering religious vocations, it might be well to present the subjects' ratings of central coeducational schools with respect to their desirability for nurturing the coming generation of priests, Brothers, and Sisters. The next tabulation presents both the single-sex and the central coeducational schools as they were chosen by the respondents for vocation purposes. Parish-school percentages were omitted in the following comparisons because they seem to be disappearing as a school type and their percentages were notably low in this section of the research.

	SCD	SSS	PCD	BSS
Single sex	81.9	82.2	87.9	90.7
Central coed	4.4	0.0	6.1	0.0

When set against the high percentage choosing single-sex education, coeducational high schools are unpopular with all subjects for the nurturing of religious vocations.

Merging the percentages of preferences among the Sisters for the private and central high schools for girls, where the faculty is almost completely female, the investigator noted that 69.7 per cent of the Sisters considered either of these two types as most conducive to vocation development. When the preferences of priests and Brothers were combined in the same way, the result was a mean percentage of 69.1, almost identical with that of the Sisters. With the data broken down into smaller categories, it was patent that priest teachers preferred the co-institutional school, which by definition is a form of administration that maintains separation of the sexes in the classroom and almost of necessity postulates women teachers for girls and men teachers for boys, except in certain difficult programming situations. The Brothers strongly favored their specialty, the private high school for boys. Second on their list of choices was another sex-segregated type, the central high school for boys. Of the Sisters teaching in coeducational schools, 66.1 per cent rated the private and the central high school for girls as most effective in promoting vocations to the sisterhoods, while 73.3 per cent of the Sisters teaching in all-girls schools considered this combination ideal for the purpose. Of the priests, 54.6 per cent rated this combination ideal for vocational stimulation, while 83.7 per cent of the

Brothers held the same opinion. Percentages are shown in Table 10.

Inspection of mean percentages in the several categories might have served as a final though inadequate basis for comparison between the respondent groups involved in the study. Correlation, however, was another statistical technique employed in this phase of the research to discover degrees of relationship between participating groups. While the product-moment method of correlation deals with both size and position of scores in a series, it is not adapted to unquantified measures that are indicated only as ranks in a series. *Rho* provides a quick and convenient manner of discovering correlations with small groups. It is also useful with larger series for exploring possible relationships (Garrett, 1958).

The data for the section on school-type preferences were suited to rank-order correlation when ranged according to rank of preferences. The number of items was small, five school types from which to choose; the categories of choice were limited to three. For comparative purposes, the subjects were paired in varying combinations: SSS and SCD, PCD and BSS, SCD and PCD, SSS and BSS, SCD and BSS, and finally SSS and PCD. Table 11 presents the ranks and the resulting correlations, several aspects of which will be discussed.

The particular interest of the present study was the relationship of high-school type to productivity in the field of religious vocations. This relationship rested on factual data supplied by schools and religious communities. Analysis of Part III of the questionnaire probed the preferences of the respondents regarding the high-school type they favored for nurturing religious vocations, as well as several other attitudinal leanings. Relationships evolving in this section were based on subjective data. A perfect correlation appeared between SSS and BSS. These two groups represented the same-sex teaching environment. The correlation of the SSS and SCD rankings was .90, as was also that of SCD and BSS. These correlations were further confirmed by reference to significant chi squares for the differences between compared groups of

TABLE 11

CORRELATIONS BETWEEN RESPONDENT GROUPS AND
SCHOOL PREFERENCES

Type	SCD	SSS Ranks	PCD	BSS	Comparison	Rho
Optimum Development of Religious Vocations						
Parish high school	4	3	4.5	3	SCD & SSS	.900**
Private high school	1	1	3	1	PCD & BSS	.225
Central single-sex h. s.	2	2	2	2	SCD & PCD	.575
Central coed. h. s.	5	5	4.5	5	SSS & BSS	1.000**
Central co-inst. h. s.	3	4	1	4	SCD & BSS	.900**
					SSS & PCD	.225
Optimum Development of Adolescent Personality						
Parish high school	5	4	5	4	SCD & SSS	.300
Private high school	4	2	4	1	PCD & BSS	-.275
Central single-sex h. s.	3	3	3	2	SCD & PCD	.975**
Central coed. h. s .	2	5	1.5	5	SSS & BSS	.700
Central co-inst. h. s.	1	1	1.5	3	SCD & BSS	-.200
					SSS & PCD	.125
Personal Preference						
Parish high school	2	3	4.5	4	SCD & SSS	.875**
Private high school	1	1	2	1	PCD & BSS	.225
Central single-sex h. s.	3	2	4.5	2	SCD & PCD	-.200
Central coed. h. s.	4.5	5	3	5	SSS & BSS	.900**
Central co-inst. h. s.	4.5	4	1	3	SCD & BSS	.575
					SSS & PCD	-.125

** Significant at .01 level

subjects. When the data were considered from the point of view of greatest percentage of choices with reference to vocation development, both SCD and SSS assigned first rank to the private school. Actual raw data in percentages are shown in Table 10. The chi square computed for these differences was .728, which was not significant. This is consistent with the high correlation for the rank assigned to the private school by the SCD and SSS groups. PCD and BSS rankings, whose correlation coefficient was a notably low .225, achieved a chi square of 3.114, just barely significant at the .05 level, yet indicative of a trend toward disagreement between PCD and BSS concerning the type of high school best suited for the development of religious vocations. Here again the data lend support to the hypothesis that environmental factors wield a large measure of pressure in the formation of attitudes and opinions.

The two groups who achieved a perfect correlation (SSS and BSS) also produced a chi square correspondingly low. The similarity of viewpoints here cuts across views dominated by the person's own sex. Hence, that similarity of teaching environment somehow conditioned the respective subjects to the view that private high schools surpassed all other types as reservoirs of religious vocations might be the explanation. It is to be noted that both the correlation coefficients and the chi squares, with their significant or non-significant relationships and differences, point only to the fact of agreement or disagreement, not to the cause of these disparities. Judgments assigning causes to various phenomena are logical not statistical conclusions.

Thus far, opinions of respondents harmonized with the factual data of the research, which they confirmed with their accumulated preferences for single-sex education for vocation purposes. All four groups of respondents (SCD, SSS, PCD, and BSS) agreed in their evaluation of this form of education as best for stimulating vocations to the religious life. Neither their sex nor their teaching environment affected the basic decision to favor single-sex education, as evidenced by the comparable percentages of choice all tending in the direction of the single-sex system. The correlations demonstrated that all Sisters and Brothers were almost unanimous in their appraisal of the relative worth of several types of sex-segregated schools for the fostering of religious vocations, but the priests charted their own course of preferences. In all four groups, however, coeducational schools were ranked last as suitable for the promotion of vocations to the religious life. With this general reaction in mind, it might be foolhardy to disregard the consensus of 668 opinions. Figure 1 illustrates the opinion profiles of the four groups.

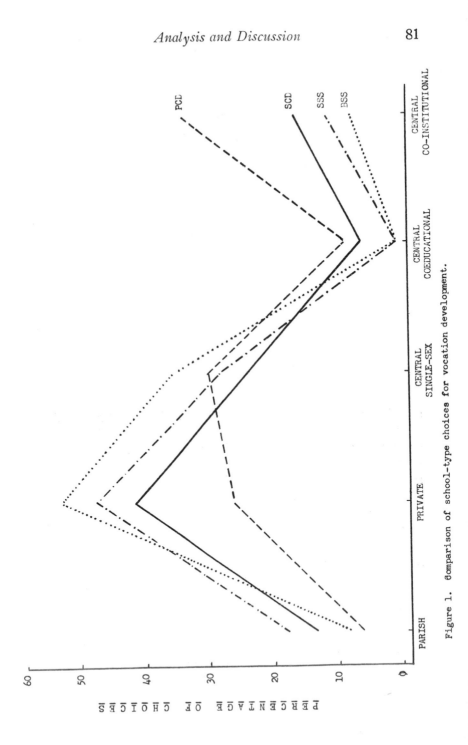

Figure 1. Comparison of school-type choices for vocation development.

While not related directly to the question of religious vocations, the areas of personal choice and optimum development of adolescent personality were treated here for completeness of coverage of the section dealing with school-type preferences. SCD and SSS showed a significant correlation in their personal preference for the private school, while differing slightly in the percentages and rankings accorded the other types. *Rho* for these two sub-groups was .875, significant at the .01 level. To strengthen the reliabilities of these correlations, chi squares were computed on the data for or against these schools. The chi square thus computed was not significant, indicating that the high positive relationships between these two patterns of choice yielded no differences that could not be explained by chance fluctuations.

PCD and BSS showed a very low correlation, as did also the groupings of SCD and BCD, SSS and PCD. It would seem from these correlations that the PCD group was little in accord with the others with respect to the type of high school personally favored. Causes of this diversity between the value choices of priests and Brothers might again be hypothesized as originating in different teaching environments, rather than in sex differences. SSS and BSS produced a significant *rho* of .90, from which it might safely be assumed that for the sample concerned, similar teaching environment is a strong factor in bringing the two sexes into close agreement regarding the high-school type personally preferred.

In the same general tenor, subjects were asked to indicate the administrative pattern they thought best suited for the optimum development of the adolescent personality. All correlations here were low and non-significant, with the exception of the paired arrangement of SCD and PCD. The *rho* for this relationship was .975, significant at the .01 level. Only once in a hundred times would it be due to chance that Sisters teaching in the coeducational system and priests primarily engaged in the same field would so closely agree in their ratings of school types best suited for adolescent personality development. While the PCD indicated through their percentage returns that they considered the coeducational and the co-institutional high schools equally suited to the purpose, SCD held the co-institutional school best for the task, with the coeducational in second place. Notable was the lack of agreement between SCD and SSS in this respect, where it would be expected that their common sex and mutual knowledge of the adolescent girl would support a greater concurrence of opinion. These data support the investigator's opinion that value choices are a function of environment rather than of dispositions related to sex.

The graphs illustrating this phase of the research clarify the close association of SSS and BSS in their range of preferences, as well as the wide divergences of SCD and PCD in their choices. The tendencies here indicated emanated from a specific teaching environment and would seem to have resulted from its subtle influences. (See Figures 2 and 3.)

Data from several other opinion sections eventuated in further confirmation of the second and third hypotheses: (a) Teacher respondents prefer teacher and student to be of the same sex for vocation purposes. (b) When teachers and students are of the same sex, the best environment is offered for fostering religious vocations. Guidance and school subjects are an integral part of adolescent school experience. When teachers and pupils are of the same sex, it is presumed that they speak a common language. Thus, in single-sex schools guidance might be facilitated and adolescents more readily conducted through problem areas which otherwise might become trackless wastes. Maher (1952) found that girls always manifest stronger preferences for more directive counseling procedures than do boys. This datum was significant at the .01 level of confidence. Group guidance which would admirably suit the needs of girls would confine boys in a personality strait jacket ill-suited to their tendencies and requirements.

Because guidance has special relevance to adolescent development and particular application to the sphere of vocation choice, the research sought the opinions and views of teachers and administrators regarding the relative effectiveness of mixed group guidance in certain specified areas. Table 12 shows the

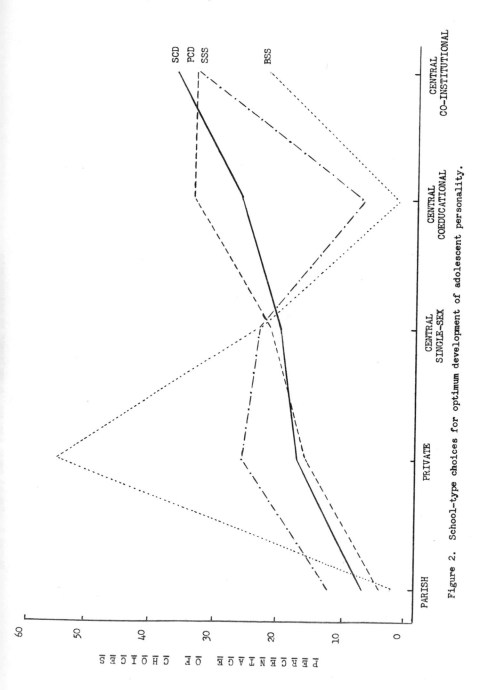

Figure 2. School-type choices for optimum development of adolescent personality.

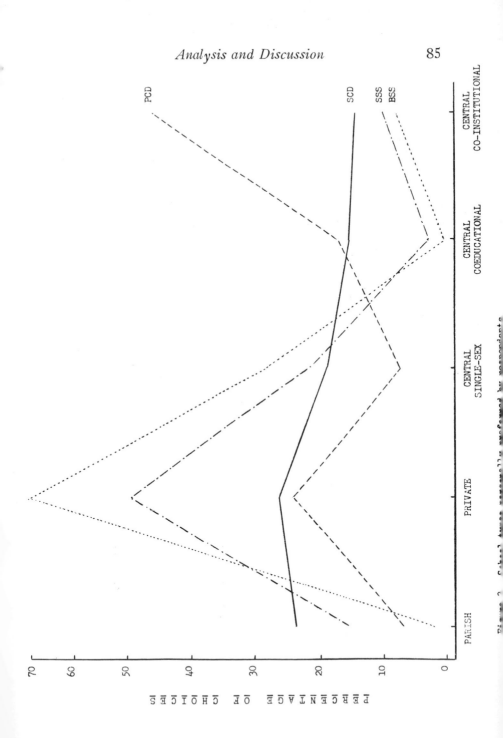

Figure 2. School type personally preferred by respondents

composite percentages resulting from the replies of the subjects. These figures represent the cumulative percentages of all replies that rated the respective item as "best explored in mixed groups."

In adolescence, greatest tensions ensue from those personality areas that are peculiarly subjective and geared to the teenager's inner concept of self, his self-image. Related to these tendencies are his attitudes toward sex, conscience, physical health, and the sense of security or insecurity with which he faces the future. But according to Table 12, just these guidance areas received the lowest ranking for suitability with mixed groups. Of particular interest are the data which show that only 12 per cent of the subjects judged guidance for vocation choice as suitable for mixed classes. Sex education for mixed groups is understandably at the end of the list. Only .5 per cent of the subjects considered it acceptable in this respect. "Guidance in moral problems" was next to the lowest rank on the list. Since vocational and moral guidance is im-

TABLE 12

GUIDANCE AREAS ACCORDING TO EFFECTIVENESS
WITH MIXED GROUPS

Guidance Area	Composite Rank Order	Composite Mean %-ages
Career Guidance	3	31.2
Sex Education	9	0.5
Personality Adjustment	5	18.9
Health Education	7	4.2
Social Graces	1	48.4
Moral Problems	8	3.5
Vocations	6	12.0
Occupational Choice	4	22.9
Use of Leisure Time	2	45.2

portant in the satisfactory adjustment of adolescent tensions, the low 3.5 percentage of educators who would select mixed groups for such guidance should give pause. It might be concluded therefore that coeducational schools do not offer adequate measures for group guidance in moral and vocational areas, unless provision is made for separate classes. When the guidance areas were ranked according to the subjects' evaluation as "unsuitable for mixed groups," their high negative *r* of -.945 indicated a great measure of consistency in their judgments.

The fluctuating percentages between the "suitable" and "unsuitable" designations were of little use except to act as a watershed for those who had definite opinions on either end of the scale. No guidance area rated a mean percentage of subject support as high as 50 when judgment was made on the basis of suitability for mixed groups. Sex education, however, was rated by 92.8 per cent of the sample as unsuitable for general patronage; moral problems, 57.5 per cent; and health education, 51.7 per cent. Stronger opinions seemed to have been expressed *against* some topics than *for* certain others as guidance material for mixed groups. The specific interest of the present study, vocation guidance, was judged unsuitable for mixed groups by 20.8 per cent of the sample. The majority of respondents judged that the suggested guidance topics could be covered, however inadequately, with boys and girls together in the group, but were preferably treated separately for maximum utility.

Rank differences were correlated for guidance areas as evaluated by the four respondent groups. Results are presented herewith:

SCD and SSS: .983)
) Based on similarity of sex
PCD and BSS: .921)

SCD and PCD: .900)
) Based on similarity of teaching
SSS and BSS: 929)   environment

These correlations are all significant at the .01 level for seven degrees of freedom. From these high correlations based on the rankings assigned to guidance areas as effective for mixed groups, the conclusion might be warranted that practically all Catholic educators included in the sample are in close accord when they regard sex education, moral guidance, and vocation counseling as incompatible with adequate instruction for mixed groups on the adolescent level.

That the field of moral guidance is one of the most crucial for the adolescent is highlighted by the fact that, by 20, he has faced more moral alternatives than his grandparents faced in a lifetime (Landis, 1940). Consequently, youth in American society today must be morally precocious to a degree not required in previous decades. Crow and Crow (1956) note that no phase of adolescent development manifests individual differences in more pronounced fashion than the area of religious experience. Boys and girls also show differences in their reaction to the transition from childhood religious concepts to mature acceptance or rejection of religious values.

Intimately connected with the problem of moral guidance then is the ordinary conduct of the high-school religion class. The assumption here is that the class in religion contributes to the guidance, moral development, and vocation growth of the adolescent. If religion cannot be taught adequately in mixed groups, then a large segment of students on the secondary level will scarcely be helped in a very important area of adolescent decision. In a related section of Part III of the questionnaire, subjects were asked to rate the usual high-school curriculum with reference to mixed-group teaching. The consensus of opinions classified biology as least suitable for mixed treatment, with religion a close second. All subjects were agreed in their estimates of religion and biology for combined classes of boys and girls. Table 13 represents their evaluations of the other subjects from the point of view of effectiveness for mixed classes.

The following *rho* correlations for each group of subjects were significant at the .01 level for nine degrees of freedom.

SCD and SSS: .977   SCD and PCD: .78

PCD and BSS: .934   SSS and BSS: .887

TABLE 13

SCHOOL-SUBJECT RATINGS FOR MIXED CLASSES

Subject	SCD	SSS	PCD	BSS
Religion	2	2	2	2
English	9	7.5	10	9
Mathematics	7.5	9	6	7
Chemistry	6	5	8	5.5
Physics	4	4	5	5.5
Biology	1	1	1	1
Latin	11	11	8	10
Music	5	6	8	8
Art	3	3	4	3
Com. Subjects	7.5	7.5	3	4
Foreign Languages	10	10	11	11

A product-moment *r* between the PCD and BSS rankings on a five-point scale was computed. The more discriminating product-moment *r* of .952 lent reliability to *rho* for all the other groups.

Lloyd-Jones (1956) reports that the Commission on the Education of Women, after studying the matter of separate curricula for them, published the following statement:

The commission has concluded that the content of women's education ought not to be different from programs of education for men. For either girls or boys, men or women, skills in reading, writing, and arithmetic bring priceless advantages; appreciation and skill in music, art, and dancing add richly to the enjoyment of life. The understanding, detachment, and objectivity that come with a thorough study of history; the appreciations, attitudes, and understanding that are derived from sociology, economics, psychology, government, and anthropology; the command and awe derived from studying the sciences; the increased empathy, sympathy, and sense of values that grow from a knowledge of literature; the sensitivities to moral and spiritual values and the appreciation of our heritage that are derived from philosophy and religion; the power of communication that comes from a command of languages—all of these know no gender. Just *how* to teach these subjects, however, so that power and understanding and sensitivity will more surely grow within the individual taught is another matter (1956, p. 252).

The implication here is that content is suited to boys and girls alike, but method calls for discernment and sensitivity to the different needs of each sex. Respondents in the present study left no doubts about their choice of school environment best suited for the optimum development of the ideals which flower into religious vocations. Vocational data and opinion data agreed that for the purpose of furthering religious vocations the single-sex is the system par excellence. Indirectly, respondents championed the same system when they rated single-sex schools superior for the more adequate guidance of the adolescent and for the more effective teaching of many school subjects, especially religion and biology, where coverage of content yields to the more weighty considerations of suitability and methodology for mixed groups.

D. *Fourth Hypothesis — Analysis*

The fourth hypothesis tested in the present study maintained that one of the strongest influences for fostering vocations to the religious life lay in the personality of the teacher. Cattell (1950) holds that the school is society's "official" and explicit institution for shaping personality to the culture pattern. He notes three chief influences in the school: (a) the personality of the other students, (b) the personality of the teachers, and (c) personality training through vicarious experience offered in reading and other symbolic references to the remote. The scope of the teacher should extend far beyond the mere implantation of facts. St. Thomas considers the human teacher a colleague on the faculty with God and the angels. Van Doren (1958) finds the teacher a crucial figure in the drama of learning for the simple reason that the student meets the subject in the person of the teacher. Whatever the teacher may teach, obviously the process occurs in the context of an interpersonal setting. This factor, more than any other, accounts for the strategic importance of teacher personality in mediating the learning process. To remove affective elements from the learning-teaching activity reduces it to sterile brain gymnastics hardly conducive to inspiring and encouraging the student.

In Part I of the research instrument, subjects were asked for the sources of their first thoughts on vocation. Of the 422 Sisters answering, 232 or 54.98 per cent considered some Sister or Sisters as the inspiration for their first vocation thoughts, while 90 Sisters or 21.33 per cent observed that a member of the family or some other mature and dedicated personality first directed their thoughts to the religious life. To the question, "If you did not enter the Community which taught you, what reasons could you give?" 65 Sisters or 52.85 per cent of the number answering this item indicated that the personal element affected their decision. While avoiding comments that might be construed as critical or derogatory, respondents were frank in their appraisal of certain defects in the members of "rejected" communities, most of their remarks centering about the lack of friendliness, kindness, and approachability discernible in certain religious. Part I also assessed the various influences that conspired in the final fruition of the vocations of the subjects. Table 14 shows those factors directly involved with personalities. Data are in percentage form.

These figures show that the greatest personal influence grew out of the matrix of school environment, since Sisters were influenced by Sisters, priests by priests, and Brothers by Brothers. *Rho* correlations between respondent groups for the 19 vocation influences suggested in the questionnaire resulted in the following significant relationships: (a) for the two groups of Sisters, *rho* (.97) was significant at the .01 level for 17 degrees of freedom; (b) for the priests and Brothers, the correlation (.531) was significant at the .05 level for 17 df.

TABLE 14

PERSONAL INFLUENCES IN RELIGIOUS VOCATIONS

Type	SCD	SSS	PCD	BSS
Nun	92.75	92.59	70.97	54.54
Mother	82.63	84.76	75.01	86.11
Father	69.36	62.50	71.88	63.63
Confessor	65.27	78.66	73.32	22.58
Companion	56.39	68.75	74.19	55.88
Pastor	49.35	42.31	77.42	25.00
Priest (Dioc. & Rel.)	42.65	36.79	67.30	12.89
Religious Brother	5.39	2.72	14.81	90.24

Respondents were also asked to judge certain factors as these contributed to the successful teaching of adolescents in high school. Of the 18 factors offered, 11 related directly to some phase of teacher personality, while the remaining seven concerned aspects of administration. Personality factors were consistently rated highest by all respondents. Only one Sister of the 504 who answered the item considered teacher personality negligible in value; all others esteemed it either essential or desirable. PCD and BSS were unanimous in their estimation of the personality factor in successful teaching. The mean percentage of respondents who rated teacher personality as "essential" to good teaching was 80.23 per cent. Of the remainder, 19.7 per cent considered it "very important."

Because most factors in the section on successful teaching of adolescents were obviously important in this respect, and since they could not therefore be validly dismissed as inconsequential, they were ranked according to mean percentages. The following factors received top ratings:

   (a) enthusiasm for teaching—89.4 per cent of the respondents

   (b) sufficient preparation time—86.7 per cent

   (c) mastery of subject matter—86.6 per cent

   (d) interest in the adolescent—81.8 per cent

   (e) personality of the teacher—80.2 per cent

It is worthy of note that four out of five respondents thought teacher personality essential in the learning process. If, as these data showed, such a high premium is placed on teacher personality in classroom teaching, it might also be so considered in the larger context of that teaching which influences intellectual and moral growth through the force of personal example.

As a correlative of the section devoted to successful teaching factors, No. 2 of Part III in the questionnaire assessed factors that might militate against the ideal "teacher image" of dedicated professional competence which should inspire youth to imitation. The items in this section were to be rated as they had been found to be a source of difficulty in the teaching experience of respondents. The factors were ranked for each of the four respondent groups according to mean percentages of choices as "very great difficulty" or "considerable difficulty." *Rho* correlations for the four groups are presented here:

SCD and SSS: .897   SCD and PCD: .781

PCD and BSS: .666   SSS and BSS: .837

The *rho* correlations were significant at the .01 level of confidence for 20 degrees of freedom. A composite of the four-fold evaluation of these problematical factors in high-school teaching ranked the difficulties according to the following order:

1. Lack of preparation time 60.94
2. Excessive extra-curricular activities 52.62
3. Inadequate guidance facilities 37.34
4. Heavy class enrollments 33.75
5. Little opportunity for professional development........ 30.36
6. Teaching technique 22.17
7. Inadequate equipment 21.12
8. Lack of experience 21.09
9. Teaching subjects without adequate preparation...... 21.00
10. Insufficient in-service help 20.87
11. Inadequate pre-service training in methodology...... 17.66

12. Subject matter 15.78
13. Lack of cooperation among faculty 13.39
14. Lack of departmentalization of subjects 11.66
15. Discipline problems with boys 9.70
16. Bright students 9.42
17. Inadequate liberal arts background 8.55
18. Inadequate psychological background 8.43
19. Timidity before older students 7.82
20. Boys and girls in the same class 7.43
21. Discipline problems with girls 4.22
22. Different religious communities on the same faculty 3.87

Inspection of the four sources of greatest strain in secondary school teaching as ranked by the respondents would indicate the possibility of their repercussion in the area of vocation recruitment. Excessive extra-curricular activities and heavy enrollment are equally exhaustive of teacher time and strength and consequently of her availability for personal consultation. Inadequate guidance facilities also point to another weak spot in the Catholic school system which may reverberate in the field of vocation choice.

A minor difficulty in the path of youth as they ponder the question of their religious vocation is the problem of personal difficulties with their teachers. Data from Part I of the questionnaire showed that such difficulty was mentioned by 9.3 per cent of the Sisters and 6.1 per cent of the priests and Brothers. Respondents noted that even though students might have no personal difficulties, they may still at times be scandalized by their teachers, with possible detriment to their vocations. Of the Sisters, 7.5 per cent considered the conduct of some teachers as a "very great obstacle" or a "considerable obstacle." The same opinion was held by 10.4 per cent of the priests and 5.2 per cent of the Brothers. These data might have represented residues from personal experiences in the lives of the respondents, since they had been asked to list major obstacles they met in the realization of their life's calling. "Scandalized by teachers" was rated as a "very great obstacle" or a "considerable obstacle" by 1.5 per cent of the Sisters, 4.0

per cent of the priests, and 3.6 per cent of the Brothers. This negative aspect of the problem, when compared with the favorable influences recorded previously, did not feature too prominently in the findings.

From the factual data gathered in the first part of the research, it was obvious that single-sex schools produced a preponderance of vocations to the sisterhoods. Causes of the great disparity might be sought either in curriculum or classroom climate. The curriculum as such is a passive medium of exchange between teacher and pupil in both types of schools. A more active element in the stimulation of vocation thoughts might be classroom atmosphere. One of the free-response elements of the inquiry raised the problem of teacher personality in mixed groups of students. Omitting the qualifying statements accompanying many of the replies, the investigator offers the opinions of the respondents about the comparative methods of teaching in all-girls and coeducational schools in the following tabulation.

Question: Do Sisters' teaching methods change in mixed groups?

	SCD	SSS	PCD	BSS
Yes	67.7 (197)	65.5 (95)	58.1 (18)	19.2 (5)
No	20.6 (60)	9.7 (14)	19.3 (6)	0.0
Undecided	11.7 (34)	24.8 (36)	22.6 (7)	80.8 (21)

In the "undecided" category were placed all responses which pleaded lack of information, insufficient experience, or which were qualified by the phrases: "sometimes," "not necessarily," and similar expressions. Most subjects maintained that the teaching methods in mixed groups changed in the direction of reduced rapport; the drop in vocations in coeducational high schools may be explainable in this way.

Sixten areas of adolescent needs were also evaluated by the respondents. Only 22.0 per cent of the subjects believed that adolescents have a great need to participate in the heterosexual social activity that dominates the coeducational system. By implication, then, about 78 per cent of the respondents believed this heterosexual association in school unnecessary and indicted coeducation, at least from the point of view of boy-girl socializing in school. Of the 16 needs suggested, adolescent socializing in school was ranked last on the list.

"Guidance in moral problems peculiar to their age group" was judged by 97.9 per cent of the subjects as a very great or considerable need of high-school students. Previously, respondents had indicated their opinion concerning the unsuitability and ineffectiveness of guidance in moral problems for mixed groups of students. If 97.9 per cent of the subjects judged guidance in moral problems an important need of students, and if only 3.5 per cent of experienced teachers and administrators considered moral guidance feasible in mixed groups, the need for separate facilities is apparent and urgent.

In addition, respondents were asked this question, specifically oriented to the adolescent girl: "Do differences in personal approach and the guidance needs of girls postulate the advisability of separate schools for them?" Results are given below:

	Sisters	*Priests*	*Brothers*
Yes	66.08 (302)	35.48 (11)	64.0 (16)
No	21.44 (98)	54.84 (17)	0.0
Undecided	12.48 (57)	9.68 (3)	36.0 (9)

Since this matter has relevance to the problem of teacher personality, it fits under the structure of the fourth hypothesis. Sisters were decidedly in the affirmative in answering the question on separate schools for girls. Although the opinions of priests and Brothers may not be statistically reliable because of the small sample tested and responding, the Sisters' replies are sufficiently representative to assure dependability. It is noteworthy that not one Brother responded with a categorical "no."

Throughout the thesis, the implication has been that environmental influences, as they prevail in the several school types, affect value choices, especially with respect to the adolescent girl's vocation decision. Factual data springing from school reports and the archives of participating congregations pointed to the confirmation of the hypothesis. From the various sections of the questionnaire, data showed the tendencies of respondents to differ in opinion and value choices as they differed in teaching environment. Sisters and priests in coeducational schools usually followed a pattern of attitudes and preferences consonant with their teaching environment and, in great part, doubtlessly influenced by it. On the other hand, Sisters and Brothers teaching in the single-sex system showed a tendency to follow a characteristic pattern of evaluation, sometimes with highly significant differences between coeducational and single-sex groups.

For further insight into the environmental influences on value choices and attitudes, the investigator sought for relationships and differences in opinions and attitudes among the four respondent groups, designated as SCD, SSS, PCD, and BSS, according to their status as male or female religious teachers in single-sex or coeducational schools. First, the Sisters in the two school environments were matched; secondly, priests and Brothers were submitted to the same procedure; thirdly, all teachers in coeducational schools (Sisters and priests) were paired with all teachers in single-sex schools (Sisters and Brothers); fourthly, all Sisters (both coed and single-sex teachers) were compared with priests and Brothers taken as a single unit. Table 15 shows comparisons for all items of Part II of the questionnaire. Mean percentages indicate degree of agreement with the respective statements, as evidenced by cumulative judgments of "complete agreement with the statement" and "strong inclination to agree but with reservations."

SCD and SSS produced few significant differences in the *General Statements* and *Vocation Aspects* sections of Part II, but *Teaching Aspects* yielded differences, three of which were significant and four approaching significance at the .05 level. Total chi squares for this comparison (SCD and SSS) were as follows: *General Statements,* 17.805, not significant for 17 degrees of freedom; *Vocation Aspects,* 17.3306, not significant for 15 degrees of freedom; and *Teaching Aspects,* 41.148,

TABLE 15

CHI-SQUARE VALUES FOR TESTS OF SIGNIFICANCE AMONG OPINION RESPONSES FOR FOUR GROUPS

Questionnaire Item	Mean %-age		Comparison	Chi Square
GENERAL STATEMENTS:				
1. Youth is the age of the greatest religious potentialities, when the capacities of the individual mature and appear in their pristine vigor.	SCD	91.67	A	.0699
	SSS	94.87	B	.0000
	PCD	93.94	C	.0000
	BSS	94.74	D	.0601
2. If young people mingle daily in their school life, any training necessary for social adjustment will automatically take care of itself.	SCD	41.29	A	.0295
	SSS	39.89	B	.1896
	PCD	45.45	C	.0000
	BSS	38.46	D	.1005
3. Intellectual and emotional sex differences correlate with deepseated constitutional differences.	SCD	68.66	A	.5340
	SSS	75.97	B	.1819
	PCD	48.27	C	2.2730
	BSS	55.55	D	.3311

Code for comparisons:

A—Sisters in coeducational schools matched with Sisters in single-sex schools

B—Priests principally in coeducational schools matched with Brothers in single-sex schools

C—All female religious teachers matched with all male religious teachers

D—All coeducational teachers (SCD & PCD) matched with all single-sex teachers (SSS & BSS)

Chi Square = 3.841 for significance at .05 level; 6.635, at .01 level. Df = 1.

TABLE 15 cont.

Questionnaire Item		Mean %-age	Comparison	Chi Square
4. Sex differences stem from differences in experience and social training.	SCD	41.61	A	.0483
	SSS	39.88	B	.1963
	PCD	37.50	C	.2441
	BSS	33.33	D	.1093
5. Coeducation harmonizes with the normal and natural relationships which prevail in the family.	SCD	63.54	A	4.7630 *
	SSS	44.61	B	6.6713 **
	PCD	68.75	C	1.7586
	BSS	20.51	D	9.4338 **
6. Close association of pupils from various parishes in central high schools weakens parochialism, the bane of united Catholic effort.	SCD	41.89	A	.0000
	SSS	41.92	B	.6667
	PCD	60.60	C	.0483
	BSS	41.02	D	.0965
7. Secondary education should provide the greatest possible equality of opportunity but not identity of instruction.	SCD	90.73	A	.1581
	SSS	95.34	B	.1171
	PCD	87.88	C	.0330
	BSS	100.00	D	.2417
8. Coeducation fosters economy of administration in teachers, in equipment, and other expenses.	SCD	72.23	A	1.0546
	SSS	62.37	B	.1456
	PCD	66.67	C	.1634
	BSS	60.52	D	1.0929
9. Prolonged, enforced association of boys and girls in high school contributes to all kinds of quaint dating patterns, etc.	SCD	63.54	A	.1583
	SSS	60.00	B	.3260
	PCD	51.51	C	.3923
	BSS	56.41	D	.1164

TABLE 15 cont.

Questionnaire Item	Mean %-age		Comparison	Chi Square
10. Broad and differential education can be found only in coeducation.	SCD	14.76	A	8.8033 **
	SSS	5.10	B	5.4902 *
	PCD	15.15	C	.5724
	BSS	0.00	D	13.2930 **
11. Coeducation injures discipline and hampers development of character.	SCD	33.01	A	.1388
	SSS	31.25	B	.6773
	PCD	24.24	C	.0654
	BSS	35.90	D	.2582
12. Our schools should make boys more manly and girls more womanly, rather than seek to equate their personality differences.	SCD	91.87	D	.2774
	SSS	97.97	B	.0000
	PCD	93.94	C	.0000
	BSS	95.00	D	.2382
13. Catholic theology unites with scholastic philosophy and common sense in frowning upon the administrative practice of coeducation.	SCD	60.96	A	1,1682
	SSS	71.91	B	.1493
	PCD	58.06	C	.0000
	BSS	69.23	D	1.2445
14. Normal masculine aggressiveness and feminine docility make fair treatment in disciplinary situations almost impossible in coeducation.	SCD	39.00	A	.0295
	SSS	40.31	B	1.3541
	PCD	21.21	C	.9658
	BSS	38.46	D	.2347
15. Under the soft-hearted regime of women teachers, boys fail to develop manly strength of character.	SCD	41.50	A	.4422
	SSS	46.63	B	.6260
	PCD	45.45	C	1.1781
	BSS	65.00	D	1.4165

TABLE 15 cont.

Questionnaire Item	Mean %-age		Comparison	Chi Square
16. Boys must be taught to act from a sense of duty and responsibility, rather than from deference to women.	SCD	84.69	A	.0739
	SSS	87.65	B	.1202
	PCD	78.79	C	.0000
	BSS	92.50	D	.1424
17. Nothing is more neglected than the education of girls.	SCD	18.39	A	.0564
	SSS	16.88	B	3.6442 *
	PCD	15.15	C	3.8264 *
	BSS	0.00	D	1.0446

STATEMENTS REGARDING THE VOCATION ASPECTS OF SECONDARY EDUCATION

Questionnaire Item	Mean %-age		Comparison	Chi Square
1. To postpone attention to religious vocations until the last years of high school runs counter to the natural and supernatural facts of the problem.	SCD	82.77	A	.4607
	SSS	90.62	B	.5181
	PCD	66.67	C	.3228
	BSS	87.18	D	.6794
2. The two most pressing problems of adolescents are vocation and sex.	SCD	86.71	A	.1496
	SSS	82.56	B	.5158
	PCD	69.70	C	.3179
	BSS	85.00	D	.0482
3. Coeducation is a positive help in developing religious vocations, since it tends to remove the romantic glow which adolescents cast around the opposite sex.	SCD	41.67	A	5.6388 *
	SSS	26.56	B	1.6678
	PCD	36.36	C	1.0596
	BSS	18.42	D	7.5408 **
4. Religious vocations to the sisterhoods are jeopardized by coeducation.	SCD	52.14	A	.0248
	SSS	50.78	B	.2192
	PCD	27.27	C	8.2796 **
	BSS	21.05	D	2.7750

TABLE 15 cont.

Questionnaire Item	Mean %-age		Comparison	Chi Square
5. Girls should not be without the influence of priests, and boys of nuns, even during their adolescent years.	SCD SSS PCD BSS	71.43 68.23 60.69 20.00	A B C D	.0837 4.5785 * 6.6872 ** 1.3896
6. Vocations to the priesthood and the brotherhoods are exposed to unnecessary risks in coeducation.	SCD SSS PCD BSS	56.27 51.79 48.48 60.00	A B C D	.2556 .1577 .0000 .0828
7. The most serious objection to the plan of separating boys and girls in our high schools is the insufficient number of teaching Brothers.	SCD SSS PCD BSS	43.05 38.02 39.39 71.79	A B C D	.4763 2.5314 2.4000 .0243
8. Some Congregations of Sisters refuse to undertake the teaching of boys of high-school age, despite the many urgent calls they receive. This is a wise measure.	SCD SSS PCD BSS	36.05 48.17 48.48 57.50	A B C D	2.9311 .1597 1.8007 3.5303
9. The natural factors of environment and teacher personality are of dubious importance in the development of religious vocations.	SCD SSS PCD BSS	21.16 19.49 6.06 2.50	A B C D	1.1697 .5350 9.5397 ** 2.1585
10. Young men are discouraged from entering the brotherhoods and persuaded to try for the priesthood instead.	SCD SSS PCD BSS	38.59 30.93 33.33 77.50	D B C D	1.6081 4.9723 * 5.0770 * 4.2347 *

TABLE 15 cont.

Questionnaire Item	Mean %-age		Comparison	Chi Square
11. Teenage dating, encouraged and fostered by the social climate of the school, sounds the death knell of many a budding vocation to religion.	SCD SSS PCD BSS	73.91 70.41 66.67 80.00	A B C D	.0805 .1311 .0370 .4089
12. Students are not sufficiently acquainted with their religious teachers outside the classroom.	SCD SSS PCD BSS	81.69 79.58 72.73 75.00	A B C D	.0195 .0000 .1464 .0379
13. When Sister co-principals must fulfill unpleasant duties as surrogates, girls form an uncomplimentary Sister image, with detriment to possible vocations.	SCD SSS PCD BSS	44.52 34.04 42.42 20.00	A B C D	2.4712 2.2977 1.4736 4.1196 *
14. The Sister-teacher's personality changes as she adjusts to teaching boys, so girls hesitate to approach her on the delicate topic of vocation.	SCD SSS PCD BSS	28.00 23.83 9.09 0.00	A B C D	.6572 1.5629 12.3850 ** 1.8988
15. Prayer and sacrifice are sufficient to obtain the grace of vocation for our students; there is no need for other methods of recruitment.	SCD SSS PCD BSS	15.02 19.69 12.12 7.69	A B C D	1.3038 .3275 1.5137 .6544

TABLE 15 cont.

STATEMENTS REGARDING TEACHING ASPECTS OF SECONDARY EDUCATION:

Questionnaire Item	Mean %-age		Comparison	Chi Square
1. When boys and girls are educated separately, each loses the stimulus and the contributions of the other.	SCD	48.35	A	4.4186 *
	SSS	33.50	B	1.2462
	PCD	42.42	C	.9549
	BSS	25.00	D	5.9498 *
2. Teachers adjust more easily to single-sex than to mixed classes.	SCD	55.67	A	3.5503
	SSS	73.06	B	.2924
	PCD	81.81	C	.0370
	BSS	70.00	D	2.5406
3. Boys and girls, separated in the learning process, may develop a superiority complex with respect to their characteristic traits and aptitudes, etc.	SCD	34.65	A	2.2880
	SSS	25.89	B	.2795
	PCD	24.24	C	1.8381
	BSS	17.90	D	3.1727
4. Single-sex classes are undemocratic and encourage a modified educational caste system.	SCD	10.13	A	1.2922
	SSS	6.25	B	2.6325
	PCD	12.12	C	.3788
	BSS	0.00	D	4.1399 *
5. The presence of girls in a classroom exercises a restraining influence on the boys and makes discipline easier.	SCD	66.23	A	3.3078
	SSS	50.25	B	4.2490 *
	PCD	69.70	C	.7175
	BSS	32.50	D	5.7868 *
6. Separation of the sexes in education is unnecessary because special classes in physical education, shop, etc. already provide for the differentials.	SCD	38.51	A	6.0886 *
	SSS	23.68	B	8.8869 **
	PCD	40.62	C	2.6621
	BSS	2.60	D	11.6556 **

TABLE 15 cont.

Questionnaire Item	Mean %-age		Comparison	Chi Square
7. If separated in the learning process, neither sex is discouraged by the particular skills and aptitudes of the other.	SCD SSS PCD BSS	52.90 61.14 67.74 64.00	A B C D	.8513 .0000 .6879 .7662
8. Single-sex classes place students in competition with others of fairly equal ability and psychological maturity, setting a really challenging pace and goal.	SCD SSS PCD BSS	59.73 79.25 53.12 81.80	A B C D	3.7702 1.2848 .0396 5.2394 *
9. Single-sex classes offer greater opportunity for more effective oral expression because the opposite sex is not present to distract.	SCD SSS PCD BSS	67.78 85.13 65.62 85.00	A B C D	2.8068 .5274 .0368 3.2880
10. Woman possesses pre-eminent powers as instructor of her own sex.	SCD SSS PCD BSS	60.21 78.83 33.33 42.50	A B C D	3.5952 .2013 5.6893 * 2.7279
11. Before adolescence, the sex of the teacher is immaterial, but with older children it is advantageous for boys and girls to be educated by teachers of their own sex.	SCD SSS PCD BSS	70.76 86.84 75.00 90.00	A B C D	2.3449 .3152 14.15 2.3837
12. Women like boys in their classes because they are highly entertaining.	SCD SSS PCD BSS	15.20 16.13 9.37 5.00	A B C D	.0647 .4563 2.3843 .0589

TABLE 15 cont.

Questionnaire Item	Mean %-age		Comparison	Chi Square
13. When either boys or girls predominate in a subject, it tends to be avoided by the minority group.	SCD	55.65	A	2.0499
	SSS	43.78	B	.7970
	PCD	46.88	C	1.2731
	BSS	32.50	D	3.7290
14. Men teachers are needed and wanted, especially in secondary education.	SCD	92.00	A	.2937
	SSS	85.37	B	.0000
	PCD	96.96	C	.2876
	BSS	100.00	D	.1634
15. The heavy female flavor of teaching staffs is a disadvantage.	SCD	60.81	A	1.5946
	SSS	49.72	B	.5189
	PCD	84.85	C	1.9427
	BSS	66.67	D	1.6696
16. Single-sex classes preclude the pressure of our culture which discourages girls from appearing superior in the face of masculine competition.	SCD	37.10	A	1.9908
	SSS	48.00	B	.0287
	PCD	25.81	C	2.2767
	BSS	28.20	D	1.6953
17. Homogeneous sex groupings enable teachers to adapt methods to the psychological needs of the group and permit wider latitude in experimentation.	SCD	81.00	A	.6172
	SSS	89.89	B	.1298
	PCD	75.00	C	.1415
	BSS	85.00	D	.6460
18. Behavior of boys in class is often unacceptable to women teachers because they fail to understand a boy's natural dynamism and aggressiveness.	SCD	70.57	A	.0832
	SSS	68.58	B	.5894
	PCD	68.75	C	.3663
	BSS	65.00	D	.2892
19. Adolescent girls frequently use their feminine wiles successfully on men teachers.	SCD	59.40	A	.1396
	SSS	55.91	B	.7840
	PCD	48.39	C	2.4022
	BSS	35.00	D	.5792

highly significant for 19 degrees of freedom. These results might indicate that although actual significance was not achieved in many separate items, the proximity to significance resulted in the highly significant additive chi square, which could mean an over-all trend toward dissimilarity of views for those engaged in different teaching environments. This lack of congruence, however, applied only to the teaching aspects, not to the general principles underlying secondary education and religious vocations, although in these latter two categories a few differences were significant.

Priests and Brothers followed the same general pattern set by the Sisters for individual items. Total chi squares for the three sections of Part II, however, were not significant at either the .05 or the .01 level, whereas the Sisters had shown a highly significant difference for the section entitled *Teaching Aspects*. When all coeducational teachers were matched with all single-sex teachers, the total chi squares for the three sections of Part II were as follows: 29.4544, significant at the .05 level for 17 degrees of freedom; 29.5472, significant at the .02 level for 15 degrees of freedom; and 55.9449, highly significant at the .01 level for 19 degrees of freedom. When

TABLE 16

TOTAL CHI-SQUARE VALUES FOR TESTS OF SIGNIFICANCE BETWEEN GROUPINGS BASED ON SIMILARITY OF SEX AND TEACHING ENVIRONMENT

Comparison	Chi Square		
	General Statements	*Vocation Aspects*	*Teaching Aspects*
SCD and SSS	17.8050	17.3306	41.1476 **
PCD and BSS	20.6588	20.1747	23.2193
(SCD & PCD) and (SSS & BSS) (all coed) (all s-sex)	29.4544 *	29.5472 *	55.9449 **
(SCD & SSS) and (PCD & BSS) (female) (male)	11.5408	51.0402 **	24.2579

** Significant at .01 level
* Significant at .05 level

all the female religious teachers were paired with all the male religious teachers, the total chi squares for each section of Part II were as follows: 11.5408, not significant for 17 degrees of freedom; 51.0402, highly significant for 15 dgerees of freedom; and 24.2579, not significant for 19 degrees of freedom. Table 16 presents the total chi square values for the four groups of respondents.

In all comparisons between the respondent groups, the greatest number of significant differences were to be found in items related to professional interests and competencies. The closest agreement between respondent groups arose in the area of general principles underlying secondary educa-

TABLE 17

MOST DISCRIMINATING ITEMS FOR COEDUCATIONAL
AND SINGLE-SEX TEACHERS

Item	Chi Square	Mean %-age (Coed Group)	Mean %-age (Single-Sex Group)
GENERAL STATEMENTS:			
5	9.4338 **	65.64	32.56
10	13.2930 **	14.95	2.55
VOCATION ASPECTS:			
3	7.5048 **	39.01	22.46
8	3.5303	42.26	52.83
9	2.1585	13.61	10.99
10	4.2347 *	35.96	54.21
13	4.1196 *	43.47	27.02
TEACHING ASPECTS:			
1	5.9498 *	45.38	29.25
3	3.1727	29.44	21.89
4	4.1399 *	11.12	3.12
5	5.7868 *	67.96	41.37
6	11.6556 **	39.56	13.14
8	5.2394 *	56.42	80.52
9	3.2880	66.70	85.06
13	3.7290	51.26	38.14

Chi Square is 3.841 for significance at .05 level   Df = 1
6.635 for significance at .01 level

TABLE 18

LEAST DISCRIMINATING ITEMS FOR COEDUCATIONAL AND
SINGLE-SEX TEACHERS

Item	Chi Square	Mean %-age (Coed Group)	Mean %-age (Single-Sex Group)
GENERAL STATEMENTS:			
1	.0601	92.80	94.81
2	.1005	43.37	39.17
4	.1093	39.55	36.40
6	.0965	51.24	41.47
9	.1164	57.52	58.20
12	.2383	92.90	96.48
14	.2347	30.10	39.38
16	.1424	81.74	90.03
VOCATION ASPECTS:			
2	.0482	78.20	83.78
6	.0828	52.37	55.89
7	.0243	42.68	43.72
12	.0379	77.21	77.29
TEACHING ASPECTS:			
12	.0589	12.28	10.56
14	.1634	94.48	92.68

Chi Square is $\begin{array}{l}\text{3.841 for significance at .05 level} \\ \text{6.635 for significance at .01 level}\end{array}$ Df $= 1$

tion. If the items of the questionnaire had been selected on the basis of greater discriminatory power, the environmental tendencies indicated in the sketchy probing here outlined might have revealed even greater and more significant differences. Tables 17 and 18 show the most and the least discriminating items for the comparisons.

Noteworthy in the comparisons between respondent groups was the greater response variation of the female religious to the different environmental influences, as indicated by the magnitude of the difference between the total chi squares for the SCD and the SSS groups in the *Teaching Aspects* of Part II.

The male religious were more evenly distributed over the range of non-significant differences. It might be asserted as a consequence that the greater female variability operates as an important tangible in various school settings, thus affecting decisions regarding religious vocations. A larger sampling and a more evenly matched group of subjects might serve to emphasize the findings of this study and bring the differences into higher relief.

CHAPTER V

Summary, Conclusions, and Recommendations

Recruitment policies of religious communities have been studied from various angles, in great part through popular literature on the subject and convention discussions related thereto. Several studies have investigated the problem and either incidentally or as a major focus of interest have studied environment in its relationship to vocation production. Invariably, the questionnaire has been the instrument most widely used. Interviews have also contributed to the fund of objective and subjective data available on the subject at the present time. The study under consideration might represent one of the first attempts to analyze statistically on a nationwide basis the relationships between types of secondary schools and productivity of religious vocations, with a special orientation to girls' schools. The research proposed to confirm several hypotheses related to vocations to the sisterhoods as these emanate from the Catholic secondary school system.

Hypotheses. The hypotheses submitted to test were: (1) Since coeducation influences girls during their most impressionable adolescent years, a relationship could be expected to exist between type of high school and productivity of religious vocations. (2) Psychological differences between the sexes would indicate that the most fruitful environment for religious vocations of students in secondary schools is offered when teachers are of the same sex as their students. (3) Teacher respondents would prefer the teacher to be of the same sex as the pupil for vocation purposes. (4) One of the strongest influences in fostering vocations to the religious life is the personality of the teacher.

Subjects. To accomplish the objectives of the study, three groups of educators (Sisters, priests, and Brothers) from the two basic types of school systems (single-sex and coeducational) were selected to represent the general population of Catholic educators in the United States. The total ex-

111

perimental group consisted of 668 subjects, of which 595 were Sisters, 33 were priests, and 40 were Brothers. Another auxiliary group, 142 major superiors of as many religious congregations engaged in secondary education, served as pivots for the investigation, for on them hinged the Sisters' name lists and those of some of the priests who participated in the research. These major superiors also contributed the data from their archives concerning the previous high-school experience of their postulants, novices, and junior professed Sisters.

Instrument. All subjects participating in the project received a questionnaire designed by the investigator. The steps in the construction of the questionnaire were as follows: (a) After careful formulation of its component parts and a review of pertinent literature on questionnaire structure, a first draft was submitted to the faculty and to a seminar of graduate students at St. John's University. (b) On the basis of their suggestions, some irrelevant sections were omitted, other parts were rephrased, and the structure modified to facilitate manipulation of the data. (c) The revised form was circulated as a pilot study among 30 persons resembling the participating population. (d) Based on the pilot study, which provided a means of evaluating the practicability of the projected research instrument, omissions and inclusions of suggested items were embodied in the final printed form. In addition to requesting data from the high-school records of the 328 participating schools, such as total enrollment, total number of vocations from 1954-1959, etc., the questionnaire also solicited opinions of respondents on various related phases of the problem on the high-school level.

Results. A. First Hypothesis. A major finding of the research was the confirmation of the principal hypothesis through the marked superiority of the single-sex type of school administration in the number of religious vocations which emanated from this source from 1954-1959. The factual data from the 328 participating schools and the 142 cooperating religious congregations seemed to indicate clearly that the relationship between type of school and religious vocations definitely exists. Of the 11 comparisons between the two types tested for significance, all were highly significant at the .01 level for one degree of freedom. Each difference favored the single-sex school.

While the single-sex type of administration as a whole was found to be the most prolific source of vocations to the religious life for women, within this system those schools privately controlled by religious congregations themselves were more productive as a vocation source than either the parish or the central high school for girls. When the private single-sex schools were matched among themselves according to enrollment categories, the schools with enrollments below 200 were found to be more fruitful in vocations than schools with enrollments according to the following classifications: 200 plus, 500 plus, and 1,000 plus. The final conclusion, therefore, is that private all-girls schools with an enrollment below 200 are most conducive to fostering vocations to the sisterhoods.

The Catholic Church, concentrating upon supernatural and moral aspects of schooling, considers coeducational institutions only second to single-sex schools. The 17 private coeducational schools in the present study showed .84 per cent vocations of their school population. However, the small number of schools in this category renders their mean percentage less stable than the mean percentage of .818 of the 82 parish coeducational high schools.

B. Second Hypothesis. Closely related to the first and major hypothesis, which postulated a relationship between type of school and productivity in the field of religious vocations, was the second which held that a greater likelihood of religious vocations of students exists in high schools where teachers are of the same sex as their students. The factual data, expounded above in favor of the single-sex school, as well as the consistent opinions of priests, Brothers, and Sisters, confirmed this second hypothesis.

C. Third Hypothesis. According to the third hypothesis, teacher respondents would prefer the teacher to be of the same sex as the pupil for vocation purposes. Teachers and administrators were in close agreement in nominating the single-sex system as best adapted to the promotion of religious vocations, especially since better moral and vocational guidance opportunities were thereby afforded the students, in their opinion. The option of the respondents almost automatically presupposed that they were also in favor of the faculty being of the same sex as the students.

D. Fourth Hypothesis. The fourth hypothesis stated that the personality of the teacher is an important aspect of vocation promotion. Most Sisters turned to the history of their own personal vocations for confirmation of the hypothesis. In addition, they expressed dislike for classroom conditions which seemed to handicap the more adequate expression of their own personality, implying thereby that the coeducational setup was least rewarding in this respect. Another grievance frequently expressed concerned the lack of rapport between girls and Sister teachers in mixed classes. When the problems attendant upon mixed classes were probed for possible sources of frustration and personality conflicts, respondents' opinions seemed divided again along the lines of teaching environment, as was evident in the analysis of other portions of the data. These situational factors, evolving from the teaching environment of the respondent groups, might be taken as the matrix of the deviations in value choices apparent throughout the research. Although in many instances the differences were not significant, they carried sufficient weight to indicate a trend, namely, that religious teachers on the high-school level resembled each other more closely in certain areas of value choices if both taught in the same kind of educational environment than if both were of the same sex. This trend might be related to the area of major interest in the present study, noting that a girl's school environment has a differential impact on vocation choice.

The configural patterns of choice of school types preferred for optimum development of religious vocations showed religious teachers in single-sex schools (Sisters and Brothers) in much closer agreement with each other than with their like-sex counterparts. The most widely divergent groups were the priests and Brothers, whose differences approached statistical significance at the .05 level for one degree of freedom. The same sex-divergent trends were apparent in school types chosen for optimum development of the adolescent personality. The differing patterns of priests and Sisters teaching in coeducational schools emphasized the possibility that environmental pressures may function as determiners of value choices.

The research instrument was so designed that it provided a large amount of opinion data, with overlapping questions to catch material which might have been omitted through design or oversight in one section or another. Since the respondents were highly cooperative, coverage was more than ample. For this reason, several sections of the questionnaire were not subjected to analysis, being deemed repetitive. Also, because the sample (668) was so large, findings might be judged reliable without need for repetitive confirmation throughout related sections of the questionnaire.

While previous investigations probed the basic notion of numbers of vocations as related to environmental and sociological factors, the present study specified more clearly the relationship between type of school and number of vocations. The research also reinforced the traditional philosophy of the Church concerning separate schools for the education of the sexes on the secondary level.

Recommendations. In general, recommendations stemming from the present study revolve about the type of school administration best suited for fostering religious vocations. The matter of administration is understandably outside the purview of the investigator's competence and authority. But were the ideal attainable for Sisters teaching on the secondary level, the research would indicate that Sisters should limit their professional activity to girls, while allotting the male segment of the student population to those better qualified by nature and experience to understand the adolescent boy, namely, priests, Brothers, and laymen. The percentage of girls to total enrollment in coeducational schools fluctuated between 51.5 and

57.6, with a mean percentage of 54.4. The vocation percentage for the all-girls schools was 1.16. If this vocation percentage were projected to the total female school population of the co-educational system, the result would be 1,386 religious vocations, instead of the 858 that were reported in the present research. The difference of 528 vocations would represent the superiority of the all-girls schools over the coeducational schools in this respect. All-girls schools postulate a female faculty, primarily religious teachers. If the Sisters now teaching the boys (100,191), who represent 45.6 per cent of the enrollments offered as data for the research, were re-allocated to the all-girls situation, approximately 2,500 Sisters would be salvaged for the teaching of girls. If these 2,500 Sisters were channeled into the single-sex schools, the number of vocations to the sisterhoods would rise. This shift of personnel would soon have repercussions in the area of men vocations also.

The study has revealed the superiority of single-sex schools for female religious vocations; it now remains to implement the facts with a program of adequate school construction and administration. Since separate schools for either sex strain already lean diocesan budgets, a compromise might be effected through wider use of the co-institutional school. This type is growing in popularity, since it serves the purposes of economy while it adheres to the directives of the Holy See concerning coeducation.

Recommendations stemming from questionnaire responses stressed the importance of adequately prepared guidance personnel and professionally competent teachers, with special mention of the personality elements which characterize the successful religious teacher. Priests in particular stressed the need for vitalizing the religion class to prepare the minds of the students for receptivity to the ideals of religious life. Sisters emphasized the need for adequate professional preparation and honored with repeated references the Sister-Formation Program now growing by leaps and bounds in the United States. Brothers concentrated attention primarily on the necessity for adequately trained guidance personnel. It will be noted that these recommendations were oriented to the professional preparation of the teacher, indicating that there might be a close relationship between teacher competency and vocation recruitment.

An untouched problem in the area of research might be the study of systematic variations of school environmental factors for boys and girls in high school. The Coleman study (1960) showed, for the sample under scrutiny, no significant differences in numbers of priests and Brothers stemming from all-boys and boy-girl schools. The present study, however, found highly significant differences for girls between single-sex and coeducational schools in the same area of research. To discover the basic cause of this discrepancy might prove invaluable for its psychological and pedagogical impact on the current practice of coeducation on the secondary level.

Another area for future study would be an investigation into the relationship between personality types of girls entering religious life from single-sex and coeducational schools. A related experimental design would involve religious communities which, as a matter of policy, teach *only* girls, and those religious communities which teach both boys and girls on the high-school level. Comparisons might be based on the numbers of vocations to the respective communities and types of schools from which these vocations stem. The topic of religious vocations would suggest still another phase of research. It might be of interest and value to investigate the hypothesis that the kind of candidate sent to a religious community by a school or parish is greatly influenced by earlier vocations from that school or parish, since "images" of the teaching Sister differ from school to school and from parish to parish. Upon this picture of the Sister depend the number and the kind of girls who follow vocations to specific communities. The problem would be to discover if a vertical analysis by parish or neighborhood over a period of about 15 years would show greater similarities in the types drawn to religious life than what might be called a horizontal analysis on a statewide or national basis, year by year. Included among the recommendations might be an experimental design with a more carefully matched population to confirm the tentative findings of the present study with respect to differences in teacher attitudes and opinions, stemming from the influences of the single-sex versus the co-educational teaching environment.

From whatever angle the problem was approached, whether factual, personal, administrative, methodological, or psychological, the answer was always the same. Single-sex schools were preferred to coeducational schools. Preferences were expressed chiefly concerning the optimum development of the religious vocation of adolescent girls, but were also applicable to various other foci of educational preoccupations, such as methods, school subjects, and guidance.

BIBLIOGRAPHY

Barrett, Sister Mary Mark. A study of the influences of Catholic high-school experiences on vocational decisions to the Sisterhoods. Unpublished doctoral dissertation, Catholic University, 1960.

Bernard, H. W. *Adolescent development in American culture.* Yonkers: World Book Co., 1957.

Blowick, J. *Priestly vocation.* Dublin: Gill & Son, 1932.

Bonney, M. E. Choosing between the sexes on a sociometric measurement. *J. appl. Psychol.,* 1954, *39,* 99-114.

Bowdern, T. S. An investigation into the environmental factors of vocations to the priesthood and the religious life in the United States from 1919-1929. Unpublished doctoral dissertation, St. Louis University, 1936.

Brown, D. G. Sex-role preference in young children. *Psychol. Monogr.,* 1956, *70,* No. 14 (Whole No. 421).

Cattell, R. B. *Personality.* New York: McGraw-Hill, 1950.

Chen, H-P. Sex differences in simple syllogistic judgment. *J. genet. Psychol.,* 1937, *50,* 3-13.

Christina, Sister M. A check-up on the problem why fewer girls become nuns. *America,* 1941, *67,* 317-318.

Christina, Sister M. Sisters supply new data on the problem of vocations. *America,* 1942, *68,* 12-13.

Cole, Luella. *Psychology of adolescence.* New York: Rinehart, 1959.

Coleman, Brother Bertram. Comparative study of boy-girl relations as a factor in the interest of boys in religious vocations. Unpublished master's thesis, Immaculate Heart College, Los Angeles, 1960.

Crow, L. D., & Crow, Alice. *Adolescent development and adjustment.* New York: McGraw-Hill, 1956.

Dale, A. Barbara. A group test of reasoning ability. *Brit. J. Psychol.,* 1926, *16,* 314-338.

Devaux, A. A. Vocation in the life and thought of Edith Stein. *Philosophy Today,* 1958, *2,* 172-175.

Diserens, C. M., & Vaughn, J. The experimental psychology of motivation. *Psychol. Bull.,* 1931, *28,* 15-65.

Douvan, Elizabeth. Independence and identity in adolescence. *Children,* 1957, *4,* 186-190.

119

Droege, J. Die Strafe im Urteil der Schüler. *Zsch. f. päd. Psychol.,* 1926, *27,* 393-407.

Evans, Brother Placidus. An investigation into the origins of vocations to the teaching brotherhoods. Unpublished master's dissertation, Catholic University, 1951.

Farrell, J., & Eileen. Vocations come from Christian families. *America,* 1952, *86,* 696-697.

Fleege, U. *Personal problems of the modern adolescent.* Washington: Catholic University Press, 1945.

Ford, T. Social factors affecting academic performance: further evidence. *Sch. Rev.,* 1957, *65,* 415-422.

Garesche, E. F. Fewer girls become nuns: an inquiry into the causes. *America,* 1941, *67,* 705-707.

Garesche, E. F. Influences in our schools unfavorable to religious vocations. *Cath. Ed. Rev.,* 1942, *40,* 286-291.

Garesche, E. F. What influences favor religious vocations. *Ave Maria,* 1950, *71,* 167-170.

Garland, Sister Mary of the Angels. Certain domestic factors in the choice of a religious vocation among women. *Cath. Ed. Rev.,* 1951, *49,* 267.

Good, C. V., & Scates, D. E. *Methods of research.* New York: Appleton-Century-Crofts, 1954.

Hagan, J. R. *Some factors in the development of religious vocations of women.* Cleveland: Sisters College, 1944.

Harris, D. B. Sex differences in the life problems and interests of adolescents, 1935 and 1957. *Child Develpm.,* 1959, *30,* 453-459.

Hartmann, G. W. Sex differences in valuational attitudes. *J. soc. Psychol.,* 1934, *5,* 106-112.

Houlahan, F. J. Trait clusters for secondary school boys and girls compared. *Cath. Ed. Rev.,* 1951, *49,* 361-369.

Keenan, A. Society and women's vocations. *Tablet* (London), 1953, *202,* 6-8.

Knoebber, Sister M. Mildred. *Self-revelation of the adolescent girl.* Milwaukee: Bruce, 1933.

Kuhlen, R. G. *The psychology of adolescent development.* New York: Harper, 1952.

Landis, P. H. Points of strain in adolescent morality. *Sch. & Soc.,* 1940, *51,* 612-616.

Leclercq, J. *The religious vocation.* New York: Kenedy, 1955.

Lindquist, E. F. *Statistical analysis in educational research.* Chicago: Houghton-Mifflin, 1940.

Lloyd-Jones, Esther. Women today and their education. *Teachers Coll. Rec.,* 1956, *57,* 431-437.

Lochet L. Apostolic purifications. *Apostolic Perspectives,* 1956, I, 17-19.

Lotz, H. R. The relationship between emotional and social adjustment and attendance at co-educational and single-sex high schools. Unpublished doctoral dissertation, New York University, 1951.

Maher, T. P. The attitude of high school juniors and seniors toward counseling procedures with reference to certain personality factors and personal problem frequency. Unpublished doctoral dissertation, Catholic University, 1952.

Mailloux, N. Morality and contemporary psychology. *Proceedings* of the eighth annual convention of the Catholic Theological Society of America, 1954, 47-66.

Mangini, Sister Rose Matthew. Professional problems of sister teachers in the United States. Unpublished doctoral dissertation, Fordham Univerity, 1958.

Mary Teresa Francis, Sister. Sources of vocations. *Sister-Formation Bulletin,* 1960, *6,* 7-12.

Masson, J. Vocations to the priesthod and environment. *Lumen Vitae,* 1958, *13,* 120-145.

McMahon, Sister Miriam de Lourdes. Religious vocational concepts revealed by survey. *Lumen Vitae,* 1957, *12,* 36-41.

Mead, Margaret. *Male and female.* New York: William Morrow, 1949.

Millar, L. *Problems in Christian education.* London: Faith Press, 1949.

Milner, Esther. Effects of the sex role and social status on the early adolescent personality. *Genet. Psychol. Monogr.,* 1949, *40,* 231-325.

Mulloy, W. J. Vocations—survey of fifty years. *Cath. Sch. Jrl.,* 1951, *51,* 132-134.

Official Catholic Directory, The. New York: Kenedy, 1960.

Schoeppe, Aileen. Sex differences in adolescent socialization. *J. soc. Psychol.,* 1953, *38,* 175-185.

Schröteler, J. Koedukation u. Koinstruktion. In *Lexikon d. Päd. d. Gegenwart.* Vol. 2. Freiburg im Breisgau, 1932. Pp. 62-66.

Sheehan, Marion T. (Ed.) *The spiritual woman.* New York: McGraw-Hill, 1957.

Shocklee, J. A. Promoting vocations in coeducational high schools. *Bulletin of the National Catholic Educational Association,* 1957, *54,* 361-362.

Spiers, E. F. *The Catholic central high school.* Washington: Catholic University Press, 1951.

Strang, Ruth. *The adolescent views himself.* New York: McGraw-Hill, 1957.

Terman, L. M. Psychological sex differences. In L. Carmichael (Ed.), *Manual of child psychology.* New York: Wiley, 1946. Pp. 954-1000.

Thienel, Sister M. Rosilda. A comparative study of religious vocations of women from various types of schools. Unpublished master's dissertation, Creighton University, 1954.

Tyler, Leona E. *The psychology of human differences.* New York: Appleton-Century-Crofts, 1956.

Usnadze, D. Das Interesse für Unterrichtsfächer bei Schulkindern in Georgien. *Zsch. f. päd. Psychol.,* 1924, *25,* 324-338.

Van Doren, M. The teacher's role in the drama of learning. *Educ. Rec.,* 1958, *39,* 199-201.

Ward, L. R. *New life in Catholic schools.* St. Louis: Herder, 1958.

Will, I. R. Rural life survey of the grade schools of the diocese of Springfield in Illinois. National Catholic Rural Life Conference, 1953.

Winkler, F. E. *Man: the bridge between two worlds.* New York: Harper, 1960.

Ziegler, Sister M. Eugenia. A comparative study of the problems, personality adjustments, and values of Catholic adolescent girls attending two types of secondary schools. Unpublished doctoral dissertation, Fordham University, 1958.

APPENDIX A

LETTER TO MAJOR SUPERIORS

IMMACULATE CONCEPTION CONVENT
371 East 150th St.   New York 55, N. Y.
                                      March 25, 1960

Dear

The vocation crisis, like a huge tidal wave, is upon us. In an effort to stem the tide, research is under way to ascertain possible reasons and remedies for the deficit. At present, I am investigating the hypothesis that religious vocations in our secondary schools are related to the *type* of school: single-sex, co-educational, and co-institutional high schools. This study is part of a doctoral dissertation authorized by the School of Education of St. John's University, Jamaica, New York, and is under the direction of the Reverend John B. Murray, C. M.

Need for this research has been indicated by Sister Mary Emil, Executive Secretary of the Sister-Formation Conferences of the National Catholic Educational Association. It is expected that the information submitted by participants will contribute in large measure to a better understanding of the factors related to vocations from our Catholic high schools.

Included in this study will be priests, Brothers, and Sisters with administrative and/or teaching experience in senior high schools. With your kind permission I hope to enlist the help of the members of your community. As respondents to a checklist-questionnaire, they will explore the vocation implications of our secondary schools from the vantage point of the administration. To ensure confidence, no signatures will be required, no community will be identified, and all data will be statistically treated. Since a proportionate and representative sampling is needed, will you favor me with a list of high schools which your community staffs, either in whole or in part? Include only such as would be ready to participate in this survey, and particularly the co-institutional high schools. These are usually not classified as such. Availabe sources of information do not distinguish clearly enough between the various types of school administration, so I must rely on your help.

As part of the survey, the enclosed data sheets are being sent to the motherhouses of teaching congregations in the United States. The information sought will help to clarify the picture of high schools as sources of vocations to the teaching apostolate. Your cooperation in completing this form will be greatly appreciated.

Since this is a national survey, data from your community are needed to validate the study. In spite of the many demands upon your time, therefore, dear   may I hope to have the completed forms returned by April 13? Data are to be tabulated early in May. The enclosed self-addressed envelope is for your convenience.

Thank you for your kind cooperation and may God reward you in return!

Sincerely yours in Our Lady,

Sister M. Celestine, S.C.C.

Approved:

Rev. John B. Murray, C.M.
Chairman, Department of Psychology

123

APPENDIX B
Data Sheet for Name Lists of Respondents

Name of Community...

Motherhouse Address ....

Please indicate the mind of your Congregation regarding the topic of co-education. Check as many items as needed to state your position clearly.

1. Specifically provides for teaching in co-educational high schools.————

2. Specifically legislates against teaching in co-educational high schools. ————

3. Provides for this exigency in broad terms. ————

4. Plans to revise present Constitutions to meet challenge of co-education. ————

5. Accepts work in co-education, but under pressure of circumstances. ————

Comment:

Please give data concerning high schools according to the following code: (1) Person in charge of your faculty members, (2) Name of school, (3) Address, (4) Diocese, (5) Number of your Community on the staff, (6) Total 1959-1960 school enrollment in round numbers, (7) Vocations to your Community from this school, 1959-1960.

FOUR-YEAR HIGH SCHOOLS STAFFED BY COMMUNITY

PRIVATE		CENTRAL GIRLS' or BOYS'	PARISH
1.			
2.			
3.			
4.			
5.	6. 7.		

Code: (1) Person in charge of your group, (2) Name of school, (3) Address, (4) Diocese, (5) Number of your members on the staff, (6) Total 1959-1960 school enrollment in round numbers, (7) Vocations to your Community from this school, 1959-1960.

CENTRAL CO-EDUCATIONAL	CENTRAL CO-INSTITUTIONAL
1.	
2.	
3.	
4.	
5.　　6.　　7.	

APPENDIX C

DATA SHEET FOR RELIGIOUS COMMUNITIES

IMMACULATE CONCEPTION CONVENT
371 East 150th St.   New York 55, N. Y.

April 30, 1960

Dear Educator:

Although religious vocations are supernatural in origin and purpose, certain natural factors have significance in their genesis, development, and fruition. Grace and nature are the dichotomy which resolves itself into the unity of the dedicated soul, called to serve God and man in religious life.

In its supernatural aspects, vocation does not lend itself to scientific analysis, yet its nature-nurture elements provide a wide field for investigation. The present inquiry is designed to ascertain the relationships of several types of secondary schools to the development and fostering of religious vocations.

Through your generous cooperation and that of many others like you, data evolving from this checklist-questionnaire will present a picture of contemporary high school life in the United States as it affects religious vocations. This study, it is hoped, will clarify the status of specific types of high school administration with respect to vocation development. Such information may have evidential value for ecclesiastical authorities and administrators as they face the future with its promise of an unprecedented growth in school plants and enrollments. A definite pattern is expected to emerge, whose outlines will be more sharply delineated through data provided by a specialized questionnaire designed for the motherhouses of teaching communities in the United States.

The need for this research has been indicated by Sister Mary Emil, Executive Secretary of the Sister-Formation Conferences of the National Catholic Educational Association. It is conducted as part of a doctoral dissertation authorized by the School of Education of St. John's University, Jamaica, New York. The study is under the direction of the Reverend John B. Murray, C. M.

Although your free time as a personal commodity is practically nonexistent, will you please help by completing the form and returning it on or before May 12? The self-addressed envelope is for your convenience. If for some reason you find it impossible to answer (or have someone else answer) the form, kindly return it as soon as you can. Every participant in this survey will add a precious bit of information to the desired whole-hearted response. You may be sure that your every effort will be gratefully appreciated.

May God reward you for your generous cooperation.

Sincerely yours,

Sister M. Celestine, S.C.C.

Approved:
Rev. John B. Murray, C.M.
Chairman, Department of Psychology

DATA SHEET FOR RELIGIOUS COMMUNITIES

Official Title of Order_____

Name and Address of Motherhouse in U. S. _____

_____ Diocese_____

Total number of professed members in your province or community_____

Final Prof._____Temporary Prof._____ Novices_____ Postulants_____

Approximate number presently engaged in teaching or school administration_____

Does your community conduct an aspirancy for students of high school age?_____ If your

community conducts a juniorate for junior professed members, in what year was it

begun?_____If you wish a copy of the statistical conclusions, please check here._____

SECTION A of the following diagram is to be filled in with the number of present postulants, novices, and junior professed, according to the type of schools from which they entered your Community. The last column is for the number of each type of school staffed, in whole or in part, by your Community at the present time.

SECTION A	Postulants	Novices	Jr. Prof.	Total	No. of Schools
Aspirancy					
Public High School					
Parish High School					
Private High School					
Central Boys' H.S.					
Central Girls' H.S.					
Central Co-educational					
Central Co-institutional					
Junior College					
Senior College					
Graduate Field					
Professional Field					
Other (indicate)					

SECTION B will show the types of high schools attended by those who entered from college, graduate, or professional levels. This section represents a further analysis of data supplied in the post-high school listings of SECTION A.

SECTION B	Entering from: Junior College	Senior College	Graduate	Professional
Public High School				
Parish High School				
Private High School				
Central Boys' H.S.				
Central Girls' H.S.				
Central Co-educational				
Central Co-institutional				

A STUDY OF THE RELATIONSHIP OF SEVERAL TYPES OF SECONDARY SCHOOLS
TO THE DEVELOPMENT OF RELIGIOUS VOCATIONS

For the purposes of this inquiry, the various types of Catholic secondary school administration are classified as follows:

1. *Parish high school:* controlled and financed by the parish, attended by boys and girls in the same classes, and taught by the same faculty, OR boys and girls in separate classes with different faculties.

2. *Private high school:* controlled and financed by a religious community, attended either by boys or girls OR by boys and girls in a coeducational setup.

3. *Central high school (boys) :* controlled and financed by the diocese, boys only.

4. *Central high school (girls) :* controlled and financed by the diocese, girls only.

5. *Central co-educational high school:* diocesan control, boys and girls in the same classes with the same faculty.

6. *Central co-institutional high school:* diocesan control, boys and girls share facilities such as library, cafeteria, gymnasium, but attend separate classes and have a different faculty.

GENERAL INFORMATION

Status: Dioc. Priest .... Rel. Priest .... Brother .... Sister ....

Educational Data: College Degree (Kind) ....

Graduate Work: (indicate) .... Professional (indicate) ....

Your present function: (check) Principal ....Co-Principal .... Asst. Principal ....

Teacher .... Counselor .... Other .... Combined administrative and/or teaching experience in terms of years .... Type of school in which you are presently situated (check first column in the following table). Specific secondary school experience in years (check second column in table).

Parish	Private	Central (diocesan)	Central (co-institutional)
Co-ed	Co-ed	Co-ed	....
Girls	Girls	Girls	Other
Boys	Boys	Boys	....

For administrative personnel only. The data sought in this section are vital to the research. Please do not omit them.

TERM	TOTAL ENROLLMENT		TOTAL FACULTY					TOTAL VOCATIONS		
	BOYS	GIRLS	PRIESTS	BROS.	SISTERS	LAY MEN	LAY W'M	PRIESTS	BROS.	SISTERS
1954-1955										
1955-1956										
1956-1957										
1957-1958										
1958-1959										
1959-1960								*		

*Tentative

PART I

Although partly personal in nature, this section refers primarily to vocational implications in the school situation. The confidential nature of these replies will be respected, and the data will lose their personal significance in their anonymity and statistical analysis. Add comments throughout the questionnaire wherever you so desire. Use additional paper for this purpose if that be necessary.

1. What was the source of your first thoughts on vocation? _____

_____

At what age did you first think of your vocation?_____ When did you finally decide upon it?

_____ How old were you when you entered the seminary or the religious life? _____

In what year? 19____ In what type of high school (see preceding page) did you receive your secondary

education? _____ If you attended co-ed schools, did these

help _____, hinder _____, have no influence _____ on your choice? What general school

atmosphere made the most impression on you? _____

If you did not join the Order to which your teachers belonged, what reasons could you give? _____

_____

2. Indicate the relative influence of *each* of the following factors in your choice of a vocation to the priesthood or the religious life. Use the following symbols.

      5—Very great influence   1—Slight influence
      3—Considerable influence   0—No influence

_____ Prayer	_____ Retreat	_____ Diocesan priest	_____ Reading
_____ Sermon	_____ Mother	_____ Religious priest	_____ Misfortune
_____ Mission	_____ Father	_____ Religious brother	_____ An advertisement
_____ Companion	_____ Pastor	_____ Male lay teacher	_____ Vocation programs in school
_____ Confessor	_____ Nun	_____ Female lay teacher	_____ Other _____

3. In COLUMN A check the obstacles you overcame to realize your vocation. In COLUMN B check those which you consider obstacles to the youth of today. All items may be checked. Indicate in order of importance, using the following scale of values:

      5—Greatest obstacle   1—Slight obstacle
      3—Considerable obstacle   0—No obstacle

A	B		A	B	
_____	_____	Health	_____	_____	Reluctance to leave home
_____	_____	Needed at home	_____	_____	Love of social pleasure
_____	_____	Attractions of married life	_____	_____	Interest in the other sex
_____	_____	Desire for independence	_____	_____	Fear of sacrifice
_____	_____	Parental objections	_____	_____	Uncertainty about vocation
_____	_____	Bad company	_____	_____	Temptations
_____	_____	Lack of encouragement	_____	_____	Fear of difficult studies
_____	_____	Personal difficulty with teachers	_____	_____	Scandalized by conduct of teachers

2

PART II

The following section contains statements regarding certain aspects of secondary education, with emphasis on single-sex versus co-educational systems. These statements contain implications for the development of religious vocations in our high schools. They may be true, false, or debatable. In the space provided, check your opinion under the appropriate symbol. Add comments wherever you think they are justified.

A—Complete agreement with the statement
B—Strong inclination to agree but with reservations
C—Inclination to disagree rather than to agree
D—Strong disagreement
X—Not in a position to judge

GENERAL STATEMENTS:

	A	B	C	D	X
1. Youth is the age of the greatest religious potentialities, when the capacities of the individual mature and appear in their pristine vigor.	□	□	□	□	□
2. If young people mingle daily in their school life, any training necessary for social adjustment will automatically take care of itself.	□	□	□	□	□
3. Intellectual and emotional sex differences correlate with deepseated constitutional differences.	□	□	□	□	□
4. Sex differences stem from differences in experience and social training.	□	□	□	□	□
5. Co-education harmonizes with the normal and natural relationships which prevail in the family.	□	□	□	□	□
6. Close association of pupils from various parishes in central high schools weakens parochialism, the bane of united Catholic effort.	□	□	□	□	□
7. Secondary education should provide the greatest possible equality of opportunity, but not identity of instruction.	□	□	□	□	□
8. Co-education fosters economy of administration in teachers, in equipment, and other expenses.	□	□	□	□	□
9. Prolonged, enforced close association of boys and girls in high school contributes to all kinds of quaint dating patterns, to early preoccupation with social life, and directly to very early marriages.	□	□	□	□	□
10. Broad and differential education can be found only in co-education.	□	□	□	□	□
11. Co-education injures discipline and hampers development of character.	□	□	□	□	□
12. Our schools should make boys more manly and girls more womanly, rather than seek to equate their personality differences.	□	□	□	□	□
13. Catholic theology unites with scholastic philosophy and common sense in frowning upon the administrative practice of co-education.	□	□	□	□	□
14. Normal masculine aggressiveness and feminine docility make fair treatment in disciplinary situations almost impossible in co-education.	□	□	□	□	□

3

	A	B	C	D	X

15. Under the soft-hearted regime of women teachers, boys fail to develop manly strength of character. □ □ □ □ □

16. Boys must be taught to act from a sense of duty and responsibility, rather than from deference to women. □ □ □ □ □

17. Nothing is more neglected than the education of girls. □ □ □ □ □

STATEMENTS REGARDING THE VOCATION ASPECTS OF SECONDARY EDUCATION:

1. To postpone attention to religious vocations until the last years of high school runs counter to the natural and supernatural facts of the problem, since it is commonly held that religious vocations dawn in childhood. □ □ □ □ □

2. The two most pressing problems of adolescents are vocation and sex. □ □ □ □ □

3. Co-education is a positive help in developing religious vocations, since it tends to remove the romantic glow which adolescents cast around the opposite sex. They see one another as they really are. □ □ □ □ □

4. Religious vocations to the sisterhoods are jeopardized by co-education. □ □ □ □ □

5. Girls should not be without the influence of priests, and boys of nuns, even during their adolescent years. □ □ □ □ □

6. Vocations to the priesthood and to the brotherhoods are exposed to unnecessary risks in co-education. □ □ □ □ □

7. The most serious objection to the plan of separating boys and girls in our high schools is the insufficient number of teaching Brothers. □ □ □ □ □

8. Some Congregations of Sisters refuse to undertake the teaching of boys of high school age, despite the many urgent appeals they receive. This is a wise measure □ □ □ □ □

9. The natural factors of environment and teacher personality are of dubious importance in the development of religious vocations. □ □ □ □ □

10. Young men are discouraged from entering the brotherhoods and persuaded to try for the priesthood instead. □ □ □ □ □

11. Teenage dating, encouraged and fostered by the social climate of the school, sounds the death knell of many a budding vocation to religion. □ □ □ □ □

12. Students are not sufficiently acquainted with their religious teachers outside the classroom. □ □ □ □ □

13. When Sister co-principals must fulfill unpleasant duties as surrogates for Principals and Prefects of Discipline, girls form an uncomplimentary "Sister-image," with consequent detriment to their possible vocation. □ □ □ □ □

14. The Sister-teacher's personality changes as she adjusts to teaching boys, so girls hesitate to approach her on the delicate topic of vocation. □ □ □ □ □

15. Prayer and sacrifice are sufficient to obtain the grace of vocation for our students; there is no need for other methods of recruitment. □ □ □ □ □

4

STATEMENTS REGARDING THE TEACHING ASPECTS OF SECONDARY EDUCATION:

	A	B	C	D	X
1. When boys and girls are educated separately, each loses the stimulus and the contributions of the other.	☐	☐	☐	☐	☐
2. Teachers adjust more easily to single-sex than to mixed classes.	☐	☐	☐	☐	☐
3. Boys and girls, separated in the learning process, may develop a superiority complex with respect to their characteristic traits and aptitudes, causing them to undervalue each other's special gifts.	☐	☐	☐	☐	☐
4. Single-sex classes are undemocratic and encourage a modified educational caste system.	☐	☐	☐	☐	☐
5. The presence of girls in a classroom exercises a restraining influence on the boys and makes discipline easier.	☐	☐	☐	☐	☐
6. Separation of the sexes in education is unnecessary because special classes in physical education, shop, home economics, etc. already provide for the differentials.	☐	☐	☐	☐	☐
7. If separated in the learning process, neither sex is discouraged by the particular skills and aptitudes of the other.	☐	☐	☐	☐	☐
8. Single-sex classes place students in competition with others of fairly equal ability and psychological maturity, thus setting a really challenging pace and an attainable goal.	☐	☐	☐	☐	☐
9. Single-sex classes offer greater opportunity for more effective oral expression because the opposite sex is not present to distract.	☐	☐	☐	☐	☐
10. Woman possesses pre-minent powers as an instructor of her own sex.	☐	☐	☐	☐	☐
11. Before adolescence, the sex of the teacher is immaterial, but with older children it is advantageous for boys and girls to be educated and controlled by teachers of their own sex.	☐	☐	☐	☐	☐
12. Women like boys in their classes because they are highly entertaining.	☐	☐	☐	☐	☐
13. When either boys or girls predominate in a subject, it tends to be avoided by the minority group.	☐	☐	☐	☐	☐
14. Men teachers are needed and wanted, especially in secondary education.	☐	☐	☐	☐	☐
15. The heavy female flavor of teachings staffs is a disadvantage.	☐	☐	☐	☐	☐
16. Single-sex classes preclude the pressure of our culture which discourages girls from appearing superior in the face of masculine competition.	☐	☐	☐	☐	☐
17. Homogeneous sex grouping enables teachers to adapt methods to the psychological needs of the group and permits wider latitude in experimentation.	☐	☐	☐	☐	☐
18. Behavior of boys in class is often unacceptable to women teachers because they do not understand a boy's natural dynamism and aggressiveness.	☐	☐	☐	☐	☐
19. Adolescent girls frequently use their feminine wiles successfully on men teachers.	☐	☐	☐	☐	☐

5

PART III

Learning involves many intangibles. This section seeks to assess certain factors affecting both teacher and student as they impinge on each other's personalities during the educative process, thus indirectly influencing vocation choices.

REGARDING THE TEACHER

1. Rate the following factors according to your judgment of their value in contributing to the *successful teaching of adolescents in high school.* Use the scale below. If you think two factors of equal importance, give both the same rating. Add any other items you think relevant. All items may be checked.

>   5—Highly important; strongly recommended
>   3—Desirable, helpful
>   1—Slight value
>   0—No value

_____ Personality of the teacher

_____ Keen intelligence

_____ Professional competence

_____ Adequate psychological background

_____ Mastery of subject matter

_____ Enthusiasm for teaching

_____ Teacher of same sex as pupils

_____ Adequate physical equipment

_____ Separate schools for each sex

_____ Interest in adolescents

_____ Patience

_____ Good humor

_____ Good health

_____ Efficient, sympathetic administrators

_____ Effective presentation of lessons

_____ Separate classes for each sex

_____ Mingling of the sexes in class

_____ Sufficient time to prepare adequately

2. Some of the following items may have placed you under strain in the classroom, thus militating against the ideal "teacher-image" of dedicated professional competence which should inspire youth to imitation. Rate these factors as they have been a *source of difficulty in your teaching experience in secondary schools.* All items may be checked. Please use this scale. Add other factors if necessary.

>   5—Very great difficulty
>   3—Considerable difficulty
>   1—Slight difficulty
>   0—No difficulty
>   X—No experience with this factor

_____ Subject matter

_____ Teaching techniques

_____ Lack of preparation time

_____ Bright students

_____ Lack of experience

_____ Inadequate equipment

_____ Timidity before older students

_____ Inadequate liberal arts background

_____ Excessive extra-curricular activities

_____ Different religious communities on
the same faculty

_____ Little opportunity to keep abreast of
current developments in
(specify) _____

_____ Boys and girls in same class

_____ Inadequate psychological background

_____ Discipline problems with boys

_____ Discipline problems with girls

_____ Heavy class enrollments

_____ Inadequate guidance facilities

_____ Lack of departmentalization of subjects

_____ Lack of cooperation among the faculty

_____ Teaching subjects without adequate
academic preparation

_____ Inadequate pre-service preparation in
methodology

_____ Insufficient in-service help

6

REGARDING THE STUDENT

1. Which of the following guidance areas can best be explored in a mixed group of boys and girls? Use these values: 5—best; 3—next; 1—least; 0—not for mixed groups.

   ------- Career guidance

   ------- Sex education

   ------- Personality adjustment

   ------- Health education

   ------- Social graces

   ------- Moral problems

   ------- Vocations

   ------- Occupational choices

   ------- Use of leisure time

   ------- Other (specify) -------- ---------------------- ---------------

2. Check as many of these subjects as you think can be taught effectively to combined groups of boys and girls.

   ------- Religion

   ------- English

   ------- Mathematics

   ------- Chemistry

   ------- Physics

   ------- Biology

   ------- Latin

   ------- Music

   ------- Art

   ------- Commercial subjects

   ------. Foreign languages

   ------- Other (specify) -------

3. Prescinding from all considerations other than *personal preference*, check in COLUMN A the type of secondary education you prefer. In COLUMN B note the type you think best for *optimum development of adolescent personality*. In COLUMN C indicate the type you consider most conducive to the *development of religious vocations*.

	A	B	C
a. Parish high school			
b. Private high school or academy			
c. Central high school for either boys or girls			
d. Central co-educational high school			
e. Central co-institutional high school			

4. Please rate *each* of the following items according to your judgment of its importance as a *need of secondary school students*. Use the scale below.

   5—Very great need
   3—Considerable need
   1—Slight need
   0—No need

   a. Opportunity to discuss problems with the teacher   -   -   -   -

   b. Opportunity to perform in class without opposing peer pressure   -   -   -

   c. Development of appreciation for cultural aspects of life   -   -   -   -

   d. Development of powers of self-expression   -   -   -   -   -

   e. Familiarity with career opportunities   -   -   -   -   -

   f. Training in the ability to think for themselves -   -   -   -   -   -

   g. Adults interested in their future   -   -   -   -   -   -

   h. Guidance in moral problems peculiar to their age group   -   -   -

   i. Chance to mingle with opposite sex in normal classroom atmosphere   -   -

   j. Opportunity to establish normal healthy friendships -   -   -   -   -

   k. Guidance in problems of personality development   -   -   -   -   -

   l. Clearer ideas about the meaning of religious life   -   -   -   -

   m. Opportunity to see teachers in an atmosphere less formal than in school   -   -

   n. Less emphasis on social activities, like proms, senior trips, etc.   -   -   -

   o. Greater emphasis on lasting spiritual values -   -   -   -   -

   p. Increased interest and practice in mental prayer and spiritual reading   -   -

   q. Other (specify) -   -   -   -   -   -   -   -

5. a) Do you think the teaching methods of the Sisters change when they conduct mixed classes? ....
Could you indicate some differences?

b) Do differences in personal approach and the guidance needs of girls postulate the advisability of separate schools for them? .... Reason (s) ?

c) Do you think that boys should be taught exclusively by men? .... If so, at what age level should this begin? .... Can you give some reasons for your point of view?

6. Please list any helps and/or hindrances to the development of religious vocations in the type of school in which you are presently situated.

7. a) By being in mixed classes, how are BOYS helped? Hindered?
b) By being in mixed classes, how are GIRLS helped? Hindered?

8. What trait (s) in the teacher do you consider valuable in drawing youth to the religious life? List in order of importance, according to your judgment.

9. a) If you see a relationship between present vocation needs and current practices in Catholic secondary education, what factors do you judge important enough to warrant thoughtful consideration?

b) Granted that these matters lie within the province of the major superiors, indicate briefly what steps you would suggest to effect a change of policy, should circumstances warrant such action.

Kindly return this form on or before May 18, 1960 to:
Sister M. Celestine, S.C.C.
371 East 150th Street
New York 55, New York